LOGIC FOR WRITERS

George Bowles
The George Washington University

with

Thomas E. Gilbert
Morningside College

D1500446

Kendall/Hunt
Publishing Company
Dubuque, Iowa

CONTENTS

Foreword by Miriam Dow   v
Preface   vii
Introduction   ix

Textbook

Chapter One. Arguments   3
  I. Arguments, premises, and conclusions, 3
  II. Analyzing arguments, 3
  III. Detecting arguments, 4
    A. Illatives, 4
    B. Aptitude Method, 6

Chapter Two. Method of Supply   11
  I. Supplying unexpressed premises, 11
  II. Premises vs. presuppositions, 12

Chapter Three. Multiple Arguments   15
  I. The arguments share a premise, 15
  II. The arguments share a conclusion, 16
  III. The conclusion of one argument is the premise of another, 16
  IV. The arguments are not connected with each other, 17

Chapter Four. Deductive and Inductive Arguments   19

Chapter Five. Evaluting Arguments   23
  I. Validity and invalidity, 23
  II. Soundness and unsoundness, 25

Chapter Six. Verificatory and Explanatory Arguments   27

Chapter Seven. Examining the reasoning in a piece of professional
    writing   31
    I. Analysis of the argument, 31
  II. Are the premises true or false?, 32
 III. Is the argument valid?, 36
 IV. Is the argument sound?, 37

Chapter Eight. Examining the reasoning in a piece of student writing   39
    I. The essay, 39
  II. The first paragraph, 41
 III. The second paragraph, 44
 IV. The third paragraph, 46
  V. The fourth paragraph, 50

Chapter Nine. Concluding advice to students   53

Workbook

Instructions   57

Exercise Set 1 (12 exercises)   81
Exercise Set 2 (6 exercises)   160
Exercise Set 3 (8 exercises)   130
Exercise Set 4 (9 exercises)   94
Exercise Set 5 (11 exercises)   168
Exercise Set 6 (8 exercises)   149

Index of Workbook Exercises   177

FOREWORD

Logic for Writers is a logic text condensed to deal with the principal characteristics of single arguments and chains of arguments. It is appropriate for Composition and other writing courses in which students write argumentative or persuasive essays and research papers. In other words, it is meant for writing courses in which the level of ideas is a crucial element. To that end, it provides an analytical method, the application of which is itself a challenging thinking process.

Of the three sides of the rhetorical triangle, this text concerns itself not with ethos or pathos but with logos (which writing teachers variously call the message, or the argument), and not with the aesthetic or even the persuasive characteristics of logos but only with its logic. Writing teachers themselves provide those characteristics, and the other elements of the rhetorical situation: the elements which give authority to the writer and those which appeal to specific audiences.

What can such a book do for our students? It can help them find and evaluate arguments, and so help them become more critical readers of challenging texts. It can help them find and evaluate the arguments in their own writing, and so help them become more rigorous writers. And it gives to both students and teachers a precise vocabulary with which to discuss student arguments, a vocabulary which does away with that familiar, frustrating dialogue:

Teacher: That's just an assertion.
Student: No—that's my opinion, and you said you wanted our views on this issue.

Logic for Writers enables students and teachers to talk to each other on the level of ideas, not emotions. It disciplines teachers to help students make their own arguments more logical, and dispels the sometimes justified suspicion on the part of students that the teacher is trying to change their minds.

Because the text is brief, it is appropriate for writing courses with a particular agenda and specific texts, such as theme, humanities, and writing-across-the-curriculum courses, in which it is sometimes difficult to use other argument texts, precisely because they come with the elaborate apparatus of the whole rhetorical situation.

Logic for Writers invites students to critical thought, and challenges teachers, in the imagery of the Renaissance, to help students clasp the closed fist of logic with the open palm of rhetoric.

Miriam Dow
Director of Writing
The George Washington University

PREFACE

This book is an abbreviated and simplified version of our unpublished logic textbook, *Everyday Logic,* and its accompanying *Logic Workbook.* As almost everything we say in this book is to some degree controversial, we do not pretend to speak on behalf of *all* logicians. Nor do we attempt to speak for *most* logicians, except when we think they are correct. We attempt to tell you only what we think is both true and likely to be useful in improving your reading and writing.

We would like to acknowledge the help and encouragement we have received from members of the faculty of The George Washington University: Miriam Dow, Tara Wallace, Jenny Varden, Palmer Graham, Eleanor Garner, and others of the English Department, and William B. Griffith of the Philosophy Department.

INTRODUCTION

Logic for Writers? What, you may be asking yourself, does logic have to do with writing? The answer is that much of what you write (and read) expresses reasoning—*i.e.,* offers reasons for things—; and logic's central subject-matter is reasoning. Logic can teach you how to detect and evaluate the reasoning of others, so it can help you to improve your understanding of what they write. And it can teach you how to express and critically examine your own reasoning, so it can also help you to improve your writing. That is what logic has to do with writing.

This book consists of two parts: a textbook of nine chapters and a workbook of six exercise sets. The first chapter of the textbook deals with the smallest units of reasoning—namely, arguments—and how to detect or express them. The second chapter shows you how to supply any of an argument's premises that the arguer has not expressed, while the third chapter shows the various ways in which arguments may be connected with each other. The fourth chapter shows you how to distinguish deductive arguments from inductive ones, which is generally indispensable to evaluating them; for deductive and inductive arguments are evaluated according to different standards. The fifth chapter deals with the evaluation of arguments: it shows you the ways in which arguments can be good and the ways in which they can be bad. Even good arguments may have fundamentally different kinds of functions, and Chapter Six treats of these when it distinguishes verificatory arguments from explanatory ones. The next two chapters of the textbook apply what you have learned in the preceding chapters to two pieces of writing: in Chapter Seven it is a piece of professional writing, while in Chapter Eight it is a student essay. The final chapter offers advice to students.

The workbook is written in a different way from the textbook. It is not designed to be read page-by-page, like an ordinary book; so don't try to read it that way. Instead, turn first to the instructions on page 57. Exercise Set One in the workbook deals with Chapter One in the textbook, Set Two with Chapter Two, and so on.

That's enough introduction. Now let's learn something about arguments.

TEXTBOOK

ARGUMENTS

I. Arguments, premises, and conclusions

The word 'argument' has several meanings. It can mean:

1. The smallest unit of reasoning.
2. The premises of an argument, in sense (1).
3. A chain of arguments, in sense (1).
4. A debate, in which opposing arguments, in the preceding senses, are considered, criticized, and weighed against each other.

Although composition textbooks usually use 'argument' in the fourth sense, we shall be using the word in the first sense—*i.e.,* the sense in which an *argument* is the smallest unit of reasoning. As such, it is a whole consisting of the following parts: a *conclusion* and one or more *premises*. These parts are related to each other in that the person who has the argument in mind thinks that the premises are *reasons for* the conclusion—*i.e.,* that the premises make the conclusion *probable* or *certain*. Whether or not the premises *actually* make the conclusion probable or certain has nothing to do with whether they compose an argument: that is determined solely by the fact that the arguer *thinks* that they do.

II. Analyzing arguments

To *analyze* an argument is to take it apart, distinguishing not only its conclusion from its premises but also, if it has more than one premise, each premise from the others. Analyzing an argument differs from evaluating, or criticizing, it in that whereas analyzing an argument is specifying what all of its parts are, evaluating it is judging whether it is good or bad. We shall return to the subject of evaluating arguments in Chapter Five.

One clear way to analyze an argument is to label its conclusion with a 'C' and its premise with a 'P', writing the conclusion beneath the premise, like this:

P. All men are mortals.
C. Some mortals are men.

If the argument has more than one premise, we distinguish one premise from another by placing numerals after the 'P', like this:

P1. All men are mortals.
P2. Socrates is a man.
C. Socrates is a mortal.

And if a text contains more than one argument, we distinguish one argument from another by labeling the arguments 'A1', 'A2', *etc.,* thus:

A1.
P. All men are mortals.
C. Some mortals are men.
A2.

P1. All men are mortals.
P2. Socrates is a man.
C. Socrates is a mortal.

III. Detecting arguments

A. Illatives

The surest way to ascertain that a text expresses an argument is by means of *illatives,* which are words or expressions that indicate that one thing is thought of as a reason for another. For instance, when the word 'therefore', which is an illative, occurs in the text—

All men are mortals. Therefore, all right-handed men are mortals.

—, it tells us not only that 'All men are mortals' is a premise, but also that 'All right-handed men are mortals' is a conclusion, in an argument. That is, it tells us that the text expresses the argument—

P. All men are mortals.
C. All right-handed men are mortals.

Likewise, the occurrence of the illative 'because' in the text—

All right-handed men are mortals, because all men are mortals.

—tells us that the text expresses the same argument. Similarly, the fact that the illative 'why' occurs in the text—

4

Smith: Why is Socrates a mortal?
Jones: He is a man, and all men are mortals.

—tells us that Smith requests a reason (*i.e.,* a premise) for the conclusion 'Socrates is a mortal'. And the fact that Jones complies with Smith's request tells us that 'He [Socrates] is a man' and 'All men are mortals' are premises. Thus, we learn that the text expresses the argument—

P1. He [Socrates] is a man.
P2. All men are mortals.
C. Socrates is a mortal.

Two or more illatives can work together with each other to point out the same argument. For example, in the text—

All men are mortals. Therefore, Socrates
is a mortal, because he is a man.

—, the illatives 'therefore' and 'because' work together with each other to indicate the same argument. 'Therefore' tells us that 'All men are mortals' is a premise and that 'Socrates is a mortal' is a conclusion. 'Because' tells us that 'Socrates is a mortal' is a conclusion and that 'He [Socrates] is a man' is a premise. The conclusion of this argument, then, is pointed out by both illatives, and each premise by only one.

Besides 'therefore', 'because', and 'why' there are such illatives as:

Since	For
As	Inasmuch as
Indicates	Assuming that
Hence	Consequently
So	If

There is even one item of ordinary punctuation that sometimes acts as an illative—namely, the colon.

Example 1.1

Text:

. . . *I think, therefore I am, or exist,* . . . .

—René Descartes, "Discourse on the Method of Rightly Conducting the Reason and Seeking Truth in the Field of Science" (1637); reprinted in *Discourse on Method and Meditations,* tr. Laurence J. Lafleur (Indianapolis: The Bobbs-Merrill Company, Inc., 1960), Part Four, p. 24.

Discussion:

'Therefore' is an illative, and its occurrence in this text tells us both that 'I [René Descartes] think' is a premise and that 'I [René Descartes] am, or exist' is a conclusion. It thus permits us to ascertain that this text expresses the argument—

> P. I [René Descartes] think.
> C. I am, or exist.

B. Aptitude method

Sometimes an arguer thinks of something he has expressed as a premise, or a conclusion, or even an entire argument, without telling us so by means of illatives. This naturally makes it harder for us to detect and hence to analyze his argument than if he had indicated everything by means of illatives. In such cases we employ the *Aptitude Method,* which tests the aptitude that the propositions[1] expressed in the text have for being premises or conclusions. The Aptitude Method goes like this:

1. If the text expresses two propositions, x and y, near each other, we ask whether one would plausibly be a reason for the other.
2. If x would plausibly be a reason for y, but y would not as plausibly be a reason for x, we conclude that the text expresses the argument—

> P. x.
> C. y.

For instance, in the text—

All men are mortals. All right-handed men are mortals.

—, 'All men are mortals' would plausibly be a reason for 'Some mortals are men', but the latter would not plausibly be a reason for the former. So, we conclude that the text expresses the argument—

> P. All men are mortals.
> C. All right-handed men are mortals.

---

1. By 'proposition' we mean neither a sentence nor a clause but a kind of meaning that is (1) expressible by means of a grammatically complete sentence and (2) capable of being true or false. 'Statement' and 'assertion' would mean nearly the same.

3. If neither would plausibly be a reason for the other, we conclude that *x* and *y* do not comprise an argument. For example, in the text—

> Some people who work in Washington, D.C. are inhabitants of Virginia. Others live in Maryland.

—, neither proposition would plausibly be a reason for the other, and so we conclude that neither is a premise in an argument in which the other is a conclusion.

4. If *x* and *y* would plausibly be reasons for each other, we conclude that whichever is expressed earlier in the text is the conclusion, and that the other is the premise. For instance, in the text—

> Socrates wears the same clothing year around. In winter, you can see him in the same cloak he wears in summer.

—, the propositions 'Socrates wears the same clothing year around' and 'In winter, you can see him in the same cloak he wears in summer' would plausibly be reasons for each other. We therefore conclude that the text expresses an argument whose conclusion is whichever of the two propositions is expressed earlier in the text. Since the proposition expressed earlier in this text is 'Socrates wears the same clothing year around', we conclude that the text expresses the argument—

> P. In winter, you can see him [Socrates] in the same cloak he wears in summer.
> C. Socrates wears the same clothing year around.

Let's see how the Aptitude Method can be applied to texts from the real world.

Example 1.2

Text:

> The act of intentionally taking a human life is murder. Since abortion is the intentional termination of pregnancy by inducing the loss of the fetus, and the fetus is a living human being, any act of abortion is an act of murder. . . .

—Carl Wellman, *Morals & Ethics* (Glenview, Illinois: Scott, Foresman and Company, 1975), p. 164. (Example found by Greg Wilcox)

Discussion:

As the illative 'since' tells us, the text expresses the argument—

P1. Abortion is the intentional termination of pregnancy by inducing the loss of the fetus.
P2. The fetus is a living human being.
 C. Any act of abortion is an act of murder.

But these two premises alone are not sufficient reasons for the conclusion. They need the help of another premise. So we search for it in the text, and we find 'The act of intentionally taking a human life is murder'. That proposition will help the other two premises as reasons for the conclusion, but the conclusion would not plausibly be a reason for it. And so, using the Aptitude Method, we add this third premise to the argument:

P1. Abortion is the intentional termination of pregnancy by inducing the loss of the fetus.
P2. The fetus is a living human being.
P3. The act of intentionally taking a human life is murder.
 C. Any act of abortion is an act of murder.

Example 1.3

Text:

It is a piece of idle sentimentality that truth, merely as truth, has any inherent power denied to error of prevailing against the dungeon and the stake. Men are not more zealous for truth than they often are for error, and a sufficient application of legal or even of social penalties will generally succeed in stopping the propagation of either. . . .

—John Stuart Mill, *On Liberty* (1859), ed. David Spitz (New York: W. W. Norton & Company, 1975), Ch. 2, p. 29.

Discussion:

This text contains no illative, but by means of the Aptitude Method we can discover the argument it expresses. The propositions 'Men are not more zealous for truth than they often are for error' and 'A sufficient application of legal or even of social penalties will generally succeed in stopping the propagation of either [truth or error]' together would plausibly be reasons for 'It is a piece of idle sentimentality that truth, merely as truth, has any inherent power denied to error of prevailing against the dungeon and the stake', whereas it would not plausibly be a reason for them, taken either separately or together. Therefore, we conclude that the text expresses the argument—

P1. Men are not more zealous for truth than they often are for error.
P2. A sufficient application of legal or even of social penalties will generally succeed in stopping the propagation of either.
C. It is a piece of idle sentimentality that truth, merely as truth, has any inherent power denied to error of prevailing against the dungeon and the stake.

CHAPTER TWO

METHOD OF SUPPLY

I. Supplying unexpressed premises

Unfortunately for the logical analyst, arguers ordinarily express some but not all of their premises. When we analyze an argument, however, we must include *all* its premises, whether expressed or not. Hence, we must use some method for supplying unexpressed premises. That method we call the 'Method of Supply', and it works like this. We come upon an argument in a text. It is obviously defective in that it is missing at least one premise. As our goal is to supply the unexpressed premise(s) that the author is most likely to have had in mind, we look for one that would (1) assist any expressed premises as reasons for the conclusion (*i.e.*, help to make the conclusion probable or certain, depending on what the author has in mind); and (2) not be likely to be disbelieved by the author. For instance, the text—

> There are one hundred senators, because each state has two.

—expresses the argument—

> P. Each state has two senators.
> C. There are one hundred senators.

—, which is obviously missing a premise. To ascertain what it is, we ask what proposition would help the premise 'Each state has two senators' as a reason for the conclusion 'There are one hundred senators' and still not be likely to be disbelieved by the author. 'There are fifty states' fills the bill, and so we add it to the argument as an unexpressed premise, enclosing it in parentheses to show that it is unexpressed:

> P1. Each state has two senators.
> (P2. There are fifty states.)
> C. There are one hundred senators.

Example 2.1

Text:

> The principle of utility is the foundation of the present work: it will be proper therefore at the outset to give an explicit and determinate account of what is meant by it. . . .

—Jeremy Bentham, *An Introduction to the Principles of Morals and Legislation* (first printed 1780; first published 1789); reprinted in *British Moralists,* ed. L. A. Selby-Bigge (Oxford: The Clarendon Press, 1897; reprinted Indianapolis: The Bobbs-Merrill Company, Inc., 1964), Vol. I, p. 340.

Discussion:

1. This text contains the illative 'therefore', which enables us to analyze the argument—

P. The principle of utility is the foundation of the present work.
C. It will be proper at the outset [of the present work] to give an explicit and determinate account of what is meant by it.

2. This argument's one premise needs some help in order to be a reason for the conclusion; for it contains no mention of the conditions under which it is proper at the outset of a work to give an explicit and determinate account of what is meant by something. But no other proposition is expressed in the text, so we cannot use the Aptitude Method to find any missing premise. Instead, we must turn to the Method of Supply and ask if there is any proposition, not expressed in the text, that would (a) assist the expressed premise as a reason for the conclusion and (b) not be likely to be disbelieved by the author. There is such a proposition: 'It is proper at the outset of a work to give an explicit and determinate account of what is meant by the work's fundamental principle(s)'. That would help the explicit premise as a reason for the conclusion, since it supplies the missing statement of the conditions under which it is proper at the outset of a work to give an explicit and determinate account of what is meant by something. And it would not be likely to be disbelieved by the author. Consequently, the Method of Supply permits us to add this unexpressed premise to the argument:

P1. The principle of utility is the foundation of the present work.
(P2. It is proper at the outset of a work to give an explicit and determinate account of what is meant by the work's fundamental principle(s).)
C. It will be proper at the outset [of the present work] to give an explicit and determinate account of what is meant by it.

II. Premises vs. presuppositions

Premises and presuppositions are apt to be confused with each other; for both are included under the term 'assumptions', so that when one tries to find the 'assumptions' of an argument, one may search for either premises or presuppositions. But only premises—not presuppositions—belong in the analysis of an argument; for an argument contains only premises and a conclusion. So, it is desirable to be able to distinguish them from each other.

A premise is a proposition that the author thinks is a reason for a conclusion—*i.e.,* he thinks that it makes (or helps make) the conclusion probable or certain. A presupposition of a proposition, on the other hand, is not a reason, but a necessary condition, for the proposition. For example, the statement 'I have seven apples', taken in isolation from other propositions, is neither a premise nor a conclusion: it is not part of an argument. But it has many presuppositions, such as 'There are apples', 'There are at least two apples', 'There are at least three apples', 'I exist', and 'Apples are the kinds of things that can be had by people'. But in the argument—

> P1. All men are mortals.
> P2. Socrates is a man.
> C. Socrates is a mortal.

—, 'All men are mortals' is a premise, since it is said to be a reason for the conclusion. But it is not a presupposition of the conclusion, since the conclusion could be true even if 'All men are mortal' were false. On the other hand, 'Something is a mortal' is a presupposition of the conclusion, 'Socrates is a mortal', and probably also of P1, 'All men are mortals'. That is, the conclusion would not be true *unless* what it presupposes were true. But the presupposition 'Something is a mortal' would not be a very good reason for the conclusion 'Socrates is a mortal', since it would not make that conclusion even probable.

Let's consider another example. The text—

> If private property were abolished, people
> would have no incentive to work.[1]

—expresses the argument—

> P. Private property were abolished.
> C. People would have no incentive to work.

If one now searches for the argument's unexpressed *premise(s),* one will find (by means of the Method of Supply) 'The acquisition of private property is people's only incentive to work'. But if one searches for the argument's hidden presuppositions, one will find, among others: 'Private property could be abolished', which is a presupposition of (*i.e.,* a necessary condition for) the expressed premise 'Private property were abolished'; 'Private property exists', which is a presupposition of the unexpressed premise 'The acquisition of

---

1. This example comes from Professor T. G. Wallace, of The George Washington University.

private property is people's only incentive to work'; and even 'There are people', which is a presupposition of both the unexpressed premise and the conclusion, 'People would have no incentive to work'. Now, it is only the premises (expressed or unexpressed), not the presuppositions, of an argument that, with the conclusion, belong in its analysis. Consequently, of this argument's "hidden assumptions", only the unexpressed premise 'The acquisition of private property is people's only incentive to work' would be part of the analysis of the argument: the presuppositions 'Private property could be abolished', 'Private property exists', and 'There are people' would not:

P1. Private property is abolished.
(P2. The acquisition of private property is people's only incentive to work.)
C. People have no incentive to work.

That does not mean that the argument's presuppositions are not important—only that they do not belong in an analysis of the argument.

CHAPTER THREE

MULTIPLE ARGUMENTS

Sometimes a text expresses more than one argument. When that happens, there are the following possibilities: (1) the arguments are connected with each other, in that they share a premise; (2) they are connected with each other, in that they share a conclusion; (3) they are connected with each other, in that the conclusion of one is a premise of the other; or (4) they are not connected with each other in any of these ways.

I. The arguments share a premise

Example 3.1

Text:

> We are genetically given our physical bodies but we *learn* the roles "appropriate" for a given sex. This means that men are actually as able as women to experience the joys of home. This also means that women should feel no more guilt than men for what is ascertained to be a neglect of duties in the home.

—Janet L. Cook, letter to the editor, *The Des Moines Register,* Vol. 123, No. 240 (February 20, 1972), p. 19c.

Discussion:

The illatives 'this means that' and 'this also means that' tells us that the text expresses the arguments—

    A1.
        P. We *learn* the roles "appropriate" for a given sex.
        C. Men are actually as able as women to experience the joys of home.
    A2.
        P. = A1-P.
        C. Women should feel no more guilt than men for what is ascertained to be a neglect of duties in the home.

—, which share a common premise. To show in our analysis that the arguments share a premise, instead of writing out the same proposition a second time for A2-P as for A1-P, we write '= A1-P'.

II. The arguments share a conclusion

Example 3.2

Text:

Legal clinics simply choose not to handle certain types of cases either because economies of scale cannot be brought to bear on them or because they are not problems often encountered by clinic clients (e.g., complex estate planning or tax work).

—Van O'Steen, letter to the editor, *Newsweek,* Vol. XCII, No. 18 (October 30, 1975), p. 15. (Mark Smedley)

Discussion:

The illative 'because' occurs twice in this text, enabling us to see that it expresses the arguments—

> A1.
>> P. Economies of scale cannot be brought to bear on certain types of cases.
>> C. Legal clinics simply choose not to handle them.
> A2.
>> P. Certain types of cases are not problems often encountered by clinic clients (*e.g.,* complex estate planning or tax work).
>> C. = A1-C.

—, which share a common conclusion.

III. The conclusion of one argument is the premise of another

When connected in this way, arguments form a "chain".

Example 3.3

Text:

Science should be taught not to spectators but to participants; therefore, we should teach computer science rather than teach *about* computer science. Thus, when one learns computer science, he is learning to deal with the kind of problems which computers are used to solve. Therefore, good challenging problems are the best vehicle for learning computing and computer science.

—Richard C. Dorf, *Introduction to Computers and Computer Science* (San Francisco: Boyd & Fraser Publishing Co., 1972), p. xi. (Chuck Hanson)

Discussion:

As the illatives 'therefore' (which occurs twice) and 'thus' tell us, the text expresses the arguments—

A1.
   P. Science should be taught not to spectators but to participants.
   C. We should teach computer science rather than teach *about* computer science.
A2.
   P. = A1-C.
   C. When one learns computer science, he is learning to deal with the kind of problems which computers are used to solve.
A3.
   P. = A2-C.
   C. Good challenging problems are the best vehicle for learning computing and computer science.

The conclusion of A1 recurs as the premise of A2, and the conclusion of A2 recurs as the premise of A3, which means that these arguments form a chain. (If the analysis seems odd to you, it is probably because the arguments—especially A2 and A3—are not very good.)

IV. The arguments are not connected with each other

When arguments are not connected with each other, they share neither a premise nor a conclusion, and the conclusion of neither is the other's premise.

Example 3.4

Text:

The Americans do not read the works of Descartes, because their social condition deters them from speculative studies; but they follow his maxims, because this same social condition naturally disposes their minds to adopt them.

—Alexis de Tocqueville, *Democracy in America,* Part II (1840), tr. Henry Reeve, ed. Phillips Bradley (New York: Vintage Books, 1945), p. 4.

Discussion:

The two occurrences of the illative 'because' tell us that this text expresses the arguments—

A1.
P. The Americans' social condition deters them from speculative studies.
C. The Americans do not read the works of Descartes.

A2.
P. This same social condition naturally disposes their minds to adopt the maxims of Descartes.
C. The Americans follow the maxims of Descartes.

These arguments do not share a premise, they do not share a conclusion, and the conclusion of neither is the premise of the other. So, they are not connected with each other.

CHAPTER FOUR

DEDUCTIVE AND INDUCTIVE ARGUMENTS

Every argument is either deductive or inductive. An argument is *deductive* if the arguer thinks or says that its premises make its conclusion certain. And an argument is *inductive* if the arguer thinks or says that its premises make its conclusion probable.[1]

Example 4.1

Text:

> Our insensibility to habitual noises, etc., whilst awake, proves that we can neglect to attend to that which we nevertheless feel. . . .

—William James, *The Principles of Psychology* (n.p.: Henry Holt and Company, 1890; reprinted New York: Dover Publications, Inc., 1950), Vol. 1, Ch. VIII, p. 201.

Discussion:

The illative 'proves that', which enables us to detect the argument—

> P. We can insensible to habitual noises, etc., whilst awake.
> C. We can neglect to attend to that which we nevertheless feel.

—, is the arguer's way of claiming that the premise makes the conclusion certain. Consequently, the argument is deductive.

Example 4.2

Text:

Though the space between the stars seems hostile to the formation of life, the evidence that organic chemistry is not unique to earth makes it probable that life exists on planets elsewhere. . . .

---

1. The definitions of deductive and inductive arguments as those which reason, respectively, from universal premises to a particular conclusion and from particular premises to a universal conclusion were suggested by some remarks of Aristotle's (*Topics* 100ᵃ25 and 105ᵃ10, ff.; *Prior Analytics* 24ᵇ18; *Posterior Analytics*, 81ᵇ1) but have not been generally employed by logicians for decades.

—"Stars: Where Life Begins", *Time,* Vol. 108, No. 26 (December 27, 1976), p. 33.

Discussion:

This text expresses the argument—

> P. Organic chemistry is not unique to earth.
> C. Life exists on planets elsewhere.

The illative 'makes it probable that' is the author's way of claiming that the premise of this argument makes the conclusion probable. Therefore, the argument is inductive.

Sometimes, as in Examples 4.1 and 4.2, the arguer uses expressions like 'proves that' and 'makes it probable that' to say whether he thinks the premises of his argument make its conclusion probable or certain. When, at other times, the arguer uses no such expressions, we assume that he thinks his premises make his conclusion certain, so that his argument is deductive.

Example 4.3

Text:

It is a piece of idle sentimentality that truth, merely as truth, has any inherent power denied to error of prevailing against the dungeon and the stake. Men are not more zealous for truth than they often are for error, and a sufficient application of legal or even of social penalties will generally succeed in stopping the propagation of either. . . .

—John Stuart Mill, *On Liberty* (1859), ed. David Spitz (New York: W. W. Norton & Company, 1975), Ch. 2, p. 29.

Discussion:

As we observed in Example 1.3, although this text contains no illative, it expresses the argument—

> P1. Men are not more zealous for truth than they often are for error.
> P2. A sufficient application of legal or even of social penalties will generally succeed in stopping the propagation of either.
> C. It is a piece of idle sentimentality that truth, merely as truth, has any inherent power denied to error of prevailing against the dungeon and the stake.

Since the arguer employs no expression to say whether he thinks the premises make the conclusion probable or certain, we assume that he thinks they make it certain. Hence, his argument is deductive.

Example 4.4

Text:

. . . I think, therefore I am, or exist, ...

—René Descartes, "Discourse on the Method of Rightly Conducting the Reason and Seeking Truth in the Field of Science" (1637); reprinted in *Discourse on Method and Meditations,* tr. Laurence J. Lafleur (Indianapolis: The Bobbs-Merrill Company, Inc., 1960), Part Four, p. 24.

Discussion:

As we observed in Example 1.1, 'therefore' is an illative, whose occurrence in this text permits us to ascertain that the text expresses the argument—

> P. I [René Descartes] think.
> C. I am, or exist.

But, unlike the illatives 'proves that' and 'makes it probable that', 'therefore' (like 'because', 'for', 'since', 'so', and many other common illatives) does not say whether the premises are supposed to make the conclusion certain or probable. Nor does any other expression in the text supply that information. Consequently, in this case, we conclude that the argument Descartes has given is deductive.

CHAPTER FIVE

EVALUATING ARGUMENTS

There are at least two ways in which an argument may be good or bad: its premises may or may not actually make its conclusion probable or certain, as the author said or thought; and its asserted premises may be true or false.

I. Validity and invalidity

An arguer thinks that his premises make his conclusion certain or probable. If they *actually* do what he thinks they do, then his argument is *valid;* otherwise, it is *invalid.* Here are some fabricated examples of valid and invalid deductive and inductive arguments:

	VALID	INVALID
DEDUCTIVE	Text: All men are mortal, and Socrates is a man. Therefore, it is certain that Socrates is mortal. Analysis: P1. All men are mortal. P2. Socrates is a man. 　C. Socrates is mortal.	Text: Most men are mortal, and Socrates is a man. Therefore, it is certain that Socrates is mortal. Analysis: P1. Most men are mortal. P2. Socrates is a man. 　C. Socrates is mortal.
INDUCTIVE	Text: Most men are mortal, and Socrates is a man. Therefore, it is probable that Socrates is mortal. Analysis: P1. Most men are mortal. P2. Socrates is a man. 　C. Socrates is mortal.	Text: Some men are mortal, and Socrates is a man. Therefore, it is probable that Socrates is mortal. Analysis: P1. Some men are mortal. P2. Socrates is a man. 　C. Socrates is a mortal.

Now here are some authentic examples:

Example 5.1

Text:

. . . I think, therefore I am, or exist, . . .

—René Descartes, "Discourse on the Method of Rightly Conducting the Reason and Seeking Truth in the Field of Science" (1637); reprinted in *Discourse on Method and Meditations,* tr. Laurence J. Lafleur (Indianapolis: The Bobbs-Merrill Company, Inc., 1960), Part Four, p. 24.

Discussion:

As we noted above, in Example 4.4, this text expresses the deductive argument—

> P. I [René Descartes] think.
> C. I am, or exist.

The premise of this argument actually does make its conclusion certain, as the author thinks, and so the argument is valid.

Example 5.2

Text:

"[Sherlock Holmes:] . . . The 'Cooee!' [that McCarthy cried] was meant to attract the attention of whoever it was that he had the appointment with. But 'Cooee' is a distinctly Australian cry, and one which is used between Australians. There is a strong presumption that the person whom McCarthy expected to meet him at Boscombe Pool was someone who had been in Australia."

—Arthur Conan Doyle, "The Boscombe Valley Mystery", in *The Complete Sherlock Holmes* (Garden City, New York: Garden City Books, 1930), p. 239.

Discussion:

This text expresses the argument—

> P1. The 'Cooee!' that McCarthy cried was meant to attract the attention of whoever it was that McCarthy had the appointment with.
> P2. 'Cooee' is a distinctly Australian cry.

P3. 'Cooee' is a cry which is used between Australians.

C. The person whom McCarthy expected to meet him at Boscombe Pool was someone who had been in Australia.

—, which is inductive, as the expression 'there is a strong presumption that' informs us. The premises actually make the conclusion probable, but not certain (since 'Cooee' could also sometimes be used by non-Australians). Therefore, the argument is valid.

II. Soundness and unsoundness

If an argument is valid and contains no false, asserted[1] premise, then it is *sound;* otherwise, it is *unsound.* So, for instance, the argument—

P1. All men are stonemasons.
P2. Socrates is a man.
C. Socrates is a stonemason.

—if expressed in the text—

Because all men are stonemasons, and
Socrates is a man, he is a stonemason.

—is unsound, because its first premise is asserted but false. But the same argument, if expressed in the text—

If all men are stonemasons, then Socrates
is a stonemason; for he is a man.

—is sound, because (1) its first premise, though still false, is no longer asserted (as the illative 'if' shows); (2) its second premise, 'He [Socrates] is a man', is asserted and true; and (3) the argument is valid, since its premises actually do make its conclusion certain, as the author believes. On the other hand, the argument—

P1. Some men are stonemasons.
P2. Socrates is a man.
C. Socrates is a stonemason.

---

1. We add the qualification 'asserted' because it seems improper to fault an argument for having a premise that, although false, was neither explicitly nor implicitly claimed to be otherwise.

—is unsound no matter how it is expressed in a text, for it is invalid: its premises actually make its conclusion neither certain nor probable.

Example 5.3

Text:

Since everything which is demanded is by that fact a good, must not the guiding principle for ethical philosophy (since all demands conjointly cannot be satisfied in this poor world) be simply to satisfy at all times *as many demands as we can?* . . .

—William James, "The Moral Philosopher and the Moral Life", *International Journal of Ethics* (April 1891); reprinted in *Readings in Twentieth-Century Philosophy,* ed. William P. Alston and George Nakhnikian (New York: The Free Press, 1963), p. 37.

Discussion:

This text expresses the argument—

P1. Everything which is demanded is by that fact a good.
P2. All demands conjointly cannot be satisfied in this poor world.
 C. The guiding principle for ethical philosophy should be simply to satisfy at all times as many demands as we can.

P1 is asserted but false. For nothing is made a good merely by being demanded. We may demand something either knowing it is an evil, or erroneously believing it to be a good. For example, we may order another drink, when we know we have already had too many; or we may insist on buying a car that later proves to be a lemon. This suffices to make the argument unsound.

CHAPTER SIX

VERIFICATORY AND EXPLANATORY ARGUMENTS

You are already familiar with the difference between *verifying* and *explaining*. It is one thing, for instance, to verify that a tire has lost air, and quite another to explain why it has. It is one thing to verify that Jack loves Jill, but another to explain why he does. Again, it is one thing to verify that light reaching us from farther galaxies is lower in frequency than light reaching us from nearer ones, but another to explain why this is so.

Verification and explanation differ in that when we verify something, it is ordinarily something not known or believed already. Often, it is something that is either doubted or subject to doubt; but when we explain something, its truth is generally not in question: it is usually known or believed already. For instance, if an astronomer verifies that light reaching us from farther galaxies is lower in frequency than light reaching us from nearer ones, it is ordinarily because someone (perhaps even himself) does not already know or believe, and perhaps even doubts, or at least might doubt, it; but if Jack explains why he loves Jill, both he and his audience normally take it for granted that he does love Jill. Another difference is that when we explain something that is caused, our explanation consists in giving one or more of its causes; but we can verify a caused event without giving any of its causes. For instance, to explain a tire's losing air is to say what caused it to do so; but we can verify that a tire has lost air without stating, or even knowing, the cause.

Now, an arguer can think either that the premises of his argument verify, or that they explain, the conclusion; and that marks the difference between *verificatory* and *explanatory* arguments. Verificatory arguments are those whose premises the arguer thinks verify their conclusions. Explanatory arguments are those whose premises the arguer thinks explain their conclusions.

Example 6.1

Text:

FOURTH PLEBEIAN
    Marked ye his [Antony's] words? He [Caesar] would not take the crown,
    Therefore 'tis certain he was not ambitious.

—William Shakespeare, "The Tragedy of Julius Caesar", ed. William and Barbara
    Rosen (1963); in *The Complete Signet Classic Shakespeare,* ed. Sylvan Barnet (New
    York: Harcourt Brace Jovanovich, Inc., 1972), III, ii, 113–114; p. 825.

Discussion:

    This text expresses the deductive argument (with the unexpressed P2
added)—

    P1. Caesar would not take the crown.
    (P2. Anyone would have taken the crown, if he had been ambitious.)
    C. Caesar was not ambitious.

The fourth plebeian means his premises to verify the fact that Caesar was not
ambitious, not to explain why he was not. Therefore, this argument is verificatory, not explanatory.

Example 6.2

Text:

Why has government been instituted at all? Because the passions of men will
not conform to the dictates of reason and justice without constraint. . . .

—Alexander Hamilton, "No. 15", in Alexander Hamilton, James Madison, and John
    Jay, *The Federalist Papers* (1787–88), ed. Clinton Rossiter (New York: The New
    American Library, 1961), p. 110. (Greg Dehnert)

Discussion:

This text expresses the argument (with unexpressed premise P2 added)—

P1. The passions of men will not conform to the dictates of reason and justice without constraint.
(P2. Government is a means of constraint.)
C. Government has been instituted.

The author intends his premises to explain why government has been instituted, not to verify that it has been instituted. Therefore, his argument is explanatory, rather than verificatory.

Chapter Seven

Examining the Reasoning in A Piece of Professional Writing

I. Analysis of the argument

In this chapter we shall use the concepts we have learned in the preceding chapters to examine the reasoning in a piece of professional writing. Here it is:

Murder in uniform is heroic, in a costume it is a crime. False advertisements win awards, forgers end up in jail. Inflated prices guarantee large profits while shoplifters are punished. Politicians conspire to create police riots and the victims are convicted in the courts. Students are gunned down and then indicted by suburban grand juries as the trouble-makers. A modern, highly mechanized army travels 9,000 miles to commit genocide against a small nation of great vision and then accuses its people of aggression. Slumlords allow rats to maim children and then complain of violence in the streets. Everything is topsy-turvy.

—Abbie Hoffman, *Steal This Book* (New York: Pirate Editions, Inc., 1970), p. iv. (John Peterson)

There are no illatives in this text, but the Aptitude Method reveals an argument whose conclusion is that everything is topsy-turvy and whose premises present seven alleged instances of topsy-turviness. In other words, the argument is this:

P1. [It is topsy-turvy that] murder in uniform is heroic, whereas in a costume it is a crime.
P2. [It is topsy-turvy that] false advertisements win awards, whereas forgers end up in jail.
P3. [It is topsy-turvy that] inflated prices guarantee large profits while shoplifters are punished.
P4. [It is topsy-turvy that] politicians conspire to create police riots and the victims are convicted in the courts.

P5. [It is topsy-turvy that] students are gunned down and then indicted by sub-urban grand juries as the trouble-makers.

P6. [It is topsy-turvy that] a modern, highly mechanized army travels 9,000 miles to commit genocide against a small nation of great vision and then accuses its people of aggression.

P7. [It is topsy-turvy that] slumlords allow rats to maim children and then complain of violence in the streets.

C. Everything is topsy-turvy.

This argument is verificatory, rather than explanatory: the author is trying to convince his audience that everything is topsy-turvy, rather than explain to them why it is so. The argument is also deductive by default: the author uses no expressions (like 'probably' or 'certainly') to tell us whether he thinks his premises make his conclusion probable or certain. So, in order to be valid, the premises must actually make the conclusion certain. Moreover, since each of the seven premises is asserted (even though in each premise 'It is topsy-turvy that' is unexpressed), the argument cannot be sound unless it is valid and each of its premises is true. So, the questions we have to answer in the remainder of this chapter are: (1) Is the argument valid? and (2) Are any of its premises false? It will be convenient to address these questions in reverse order.

II. Are the premises true or false?

Before we can ascertain whether any of the premises is false, we must ascertain what the author means by 'topsy-turvy'; for each of the premises asserts that something or other is topsy-turvy. To accord with ordinary English, he would have to mean either (1) upside down or (2) "in a state where proper or normal . . . values, [or] standards . . . are reversed",[1] or inverted. Clearly the first of these meanings is literally inapplicable to the subject-matter of the seven premises. The second meaning is applicable to some but not to others. For premises P4 ('[It is topsy-turvy that] politicians conspire to create police riots and the victims are convicted in the courts') and P5 ('[It is topsy-turvy that] students are gunned down and then indicted by suburban grand juries as the trouble-makers') present pairs of putative instances in which proper or normal values or standards are violated; but the rest do not. In P1, P2, P3, P6, and P7 respectively, it is not an inversion

---

1. *Webster's Third New International Dictionary of the English Language,* ed. Philip Babcock Gove (Springfield, Massachusetts: G. & C. Merriam Company, 1966), p. 2411.

of proper or normal values or standards that murder in costume be a crime, that forgers end up in jail, that the United States accuse North Vietnam of aggression, or that slumlords complain of violence in the streets. It seems more likely that the author has in mind a meaning for 'topsy-turvy' that, although it diverges from ordinary English, at least applies to all his premises. That meaning is probably *incongruity,* or *inconsistency.* In accordance with this suggestion, P1 would say that it is incongruous for murder in uniform to be heroic, while murder in costume is a crime; P2 would say that it is incongruous for false advertisements to win awards, while forgers end up in jail; and so on. We shall adopt this interpretation, although 'incongruous' is not a dictionary definition of 'topsy-turvy'.

In each premise, three propositions are asserted. For, since each premise has the general form 'It is topsy-turvy that both x and y', to assert each premise is to assert not only 'It is topsy-turvy that both x and y' but also 'x' and 'y'. So, each premise will be false if 'x' is false, if 'y' is false, or if 'It is topsy-turvy that both x and y' is false. Consequently, to ascertain whether any premise is false, we must critically examine not only the seven premises but also their constituent pairs of propositions.

P1 says that *it is incongruous that murder in uniform is heroic, whereas in a costume it is a crime.* The author probably does not mean to assert, on his own behalf, that murder in uniform is heroic but in a costume criminal; rather, he probably means to say that murder in uniform is *regarded as* heroic, whereas in a costume it is *regarded as* criminal. Moreover, he probably also has it in mind that *the same people* regard murder in uniform as heroic and murder in costume as criminal. By 'murder' he probably does not mean the *unlawful,* but the *unjustified,* killing of a human being; otherwise, 'murder in a costume is a crime' would be a tautology. And when he says that the unjustified killing of a human being by someone in a uniform is regarded as heroic, he probably does not mean that the killing is regarded as unjustified by the same people who regard it as heroic.

(a) Is the unjustified killing of a human being by someone in a uniform regarded as heroic by people who do not believe that it is unjustified? That depends on whether the author means that it is so *sometimes, often,* or *always.* Surely the unjustified killing of a human being by someone in a uniform is *sometimes* regarded as heroic by people who do not believe it to be unjustified; certainly not *always;* perhaps *often*—but, then again, perhaps not. Hence, in the absence of better evidence, we shall assume that he means *at least sometimes.* Then it seems that the first assertion the author makes in P1—namely, that the unjustified killing of a human being by someone in a uniform is at least sometimes regarded as heroic by people who do not believe that it is unjustified—is true.

(b) The second proposition that the author asserts in P1 is that the unjustified killing of a human being by someone in a costume is regarded as a crime. Is that assertion true or false? It depends on whether he means that it is so regarded *sometimes, often,* or *always.* Certainly it is *sometimes* so regarded; probably *often;* but probably not *always.* Therefore, we shall assume that he means *at least sometimes.* And it is true that the unjustified killing of a human being by someone in a costume is at least sometimes regarded as a crime. So, the second proposition that the author asserts in P1 is true.

The two component propositions in P1 are true. (c) Now, how about the whole premise? Is it indeed incongruous both that the unjustified killing of a human being by someone in a uniform is at least sometimes regarded as heroic by people who do not believe that it is unjustified and that the unjustified killing of a human being by someone in a costume is at least sometimes regarded *by the same people* as a crime? It would be, in a sense, incongruous or inconsistent for the same people to recognize unjustifiable killing in some cases but not in others; for a difference only in the clothing that the killer wears makes no difference to whether the killing is justified. Therefore, P1 is true.

P2 says that *it is incongruous that false advertisements win awards, whereas forgers end up in jail.* (a) Is it true that (some) false advertisements win awards? We don't know, but we would guess that some probably have. (b) Is it true that (some) forgers end up in jail? Yes. Finally, (c) is it incongruous that (some) false advertisements win awards, whereas (some) forgers end up in jail? Since false advertising and forgery are both instances of deception for advantage, and since such deception is wrong and the deceiver blameworthy, it does seem incongruous that, while some of those who commit forgery are properly punished by being jailed, some who falsely advertise are improperly rewarded by receiving awards. Thus, P2 is probably true.

P3 says that *it is incongruous that inflated prices guarantee large profits while shoplifters are punished.* (a) Is it true that (some) inflated prices guarantee large profits? Probably. (b) Is it true that (some) shoplifters are punished? Yes. (c) Is it incongruous that (some) inflated prices guarantee large profits while (some) shoplifters are punished? While there is a superficial similarity between a merchant's profiting from inflated prices and a shoplifter's profiting from stealing merchandise, there is a pronounced and relevant difference between them: the shoplifter is stealing, but the merchant is not: the merchant sells (if at all) with the uncoerced consent of the customer, whereas the shoplifter steals without the consent of the merchant. Because of this difference between the two cases, there seems no reason for the merchant and shoplifter to be treated similarly. If customers are able and willing to pay inflated prices and thereby guarantee large profits for the merchant, that is not something for which the merchant should be punished. Therefore, it is not incongruous that inflated prices guarantee large profits while shoplifters are punished, so that P3 is false.

P4 says that *it is incongruous that politicians conspire to create police riots and the victims are convicted in the courts.* (a) Do (some) politicians conspire to create police riots? That depends on what a *police riot* is. Is it a riot some or all of whose participants are policemen? No. Is it a riot resisted or controlled by police? That's more likely, although it strangely makes all non-police riots ones that are neither resisted nor controlled by police. For want of a better interpretation, let us suppose this is what the author means by 'police riot'. Now, do some politicians conspire to create riots that the police resist or control? We don't know, but we doubt it, on the grounds that politicians do not generally have the power and inclination to bring about such riots. (b) Are (some of) the victims of riots that are resisted or controlled by police convicted in the courts? Who are the victims of a riot? Strictly speaking, the victims of a riot ought to be any against whom the riot is directed. But the author might mean any who are harmed by a riot, which would include not only its intended victims but also bystanders, police, and even rioters. This latter alternative is the more probable, as it would be more likely that rioters or bystanders would be convicted in the courts than those against whom the riot was directed. If this is what the author means by the "victims", then it is probably true that (some of) the victims of riots that are resisted or controlled by police are convicted in the courts; for rioters are often, and bystanders sometimes, convicted. (c) Is it incongruous that politicians conspire to create riots resisted or controlled by police, while any harmed by such riots are convicted in the courts? It would be, if the victims were bystanders; for then the presumably innocent bystanders would suffer punishment deserved by the politicians. In sum, P4 is probably false, since it is probably false that politicians conspire to create riots that are resisted or controlled by police.

P5 says that *it is incongruous that students are gunned down and then indicted by suburban grand juries as the trouble-makers.* (a) Is it true that (some) presumably innocent students are gunned down? Yes. (b) Is it true that the same students are then indicted by suburban grand juries as the trouble-makers. We don't know, but it seems unlikely, particularly since the juries are precisely identified as "suburban": the more precise and restrictive the description, the lower the likelihood of truth.[2] (c) Is it incongruous that (some) presumably innocent students are gunned down and then indicted by suburban juries as the trouble-makers? Yes. Hence, P5 is probably false, because of our negative answer to (b).

P6 says that *it is incongruous that a modern, highly mechanized army travels 9,000 miles to commit genocide against a small nation of great vision and then accuses its people of aggression.* The "modern, highly mechanized army" referred to is probably the U.S. Army, and the "small nation of great vision" is probably North Vietnam. (a) Does the U.S. Army travel 9,000 miles to commit genocide against North Vietnam? No. The U.S. Army may have traveled 9,000 miles to southeast Asia, but not for the purpose of committing genocide. (b) Does the U.S. Army then (*i.e.,* subsequently) accuse the people

---

2. For example, the following three propositions offer progressively more restrictive descriptions and so at the same time become less probable: (1) 'Someone is at the door', (2) 'A male five feet, ten inches high and weighing 148 pounds is at the door', (3) 'A twenty-nine year-old male five feet, ten inches high, weighing 148 pounds, and carrying thirteen confused young cats in a burlap bag is at the door'.

of North Vietnam of aggression? Probably so. Since aggression is the initiation of hostile actions, the judgment comes within the purview of the Army; and since the U.S. was criticized for the presence of its Army in Vietnam, there was occasion for such a statement. (c) Is it incongruous that the U.S. Army travels 9,000 miles to commit genocide against North Vietnam and then accuse the people of North Vietnam of aggression? Not at all, since it is *possible* that the U.S. Army would intend to wipe out the people of North Vietnam precisely because they were aggressors. (The description 'of great vision' does not alter the case; an aggressive people may have a "great vision" of conquest and rule.) For two reasons, then, P6 is false.

Finally, P7 says that *it is incongruous that slumlords allow rats to maim children and then complain of violence in the streets.* (a) Is it true that slumlords allow rats to maim children? Probably not, since 'maim' "implies the loss or destruction of the usefulness of a limb or member"[3], whereas it is unlikely that rats alone injure children so gravely. (b) Is it true that slumlords then (*i.e.,* subsequently) complain of violence in the streets? Probably. (c) Is it incongruous that slumlords allow rats to maim children and then complain of violence in the streets? No, for it is not incongruous to do or permit one evil while complaining of another; otherwise nearly all complaint would be incongruous. Therefore, P7 too is false.

To conclude our investigation into the truth or falsity of the argument's premises: of the seven premises, P1 is true, P2 is probably true, and the remainder are probably false.

III. Is the argument valid?

Now, is the argument valid? No. For since the argument is deductive, to be valid its premises would have to make its conclusion certain. But even if the seven premises were all true, they would not make the conclusion certain: the fact (if it were a fact) that seven things are topsy-turvy would not prove (*i.e.,* make it certain) that everything is topsy-turvy. For it would still be possible that some things are not topsy-turvy. Therefore, the argument is invalid. (Moreover, it would have been invalid even if it had been inductive; for seven things' being topsy-turvy would not make it even probable that everything is topsy-turvy: seven is too small a part of everything.) Therefore, the argument is invalid.

---

3. *Webster's Third New International Dictionary,* p. 1362.

IV. Is the argument sound?

The argument, then, is unsound on two grounds: first, some of its premises are asserted but false; and second, it is invalid.

There, now we have done what we set out to do in this chapter. As this examination shows, sometimes substantial, but not insuperable, difficulties stand in the way of ascertaining whether an argument's asserted premises are true or false. We must sometimes guess at the meaning of an author who did not express himself clearly, and we must sometimes assess the true or falsity of a premise on the basis of probabilities rather than certainties.

CHAPTER EIGHT

EXAMINING THE REASONING IN A PIECE OF STUDENT WRITING

In the preceding chapter, we used the concepts of earlier chapters to examine the reasoning in a brief piece of professional writing. In this chapter, we shall do the same thing with a student essay, this time occasionally indicating how we would point out to the author the problems with her reasoning and what she might do to avoid them.

I. The essay

Here is the essay, with sentence numbers inserted to facilitate later reference:

Why Women Should Not Be Drafted in the Armed Forces

[1] With the controversy over the proposal for the drafting of women in the armed forces, it is no surprise that there are different opinions from many. [2] However, I feel that women should not be drafted, because they are second class citizens, they are not as physically strong as men, and they play a nurturing role to children.

[3] Women are considered second class citizens, as the role they play in society is inferior to the role men play. [4] For example, men possess the decision-making positions, such as controller over our government and economy. [5] Although women have run for public office, no woman has ever been Vice-President or President; only a few hold positions in our legislature. [6] If women are drafted, our society will have to be more lenient towards women, by giving them more authority and power in the decision-making of our government. [7] As the Equal Rights for Women has not been ratified in all states, women should refuse to register for the draft. [8] Despite the high percentage of working women, few hold executive or managerial positons [sic]. [9] A third of the working women in the United States hold clerical jobs such as a secretary, a file clerk, and a telephone operator. [10] In general, women receive sixty per cent of pay men receive for the same work. [11] With the ratification

of the Equal Rights Amendment for women, Congress would have no alternative but to grant women the same pay as men for the same work.

[12] The female's physical characteristics are different from the male's physical characteristics as the female body is structured differently. [13] The female body is not structured to render physically demanding work. [14] Being drafted in the military, women would not be able to perform some of the tasks men perform because women are usually less powerful and smaller. [15] Furthermore, women are known to be more emotional then [sic] men because women panic easily. [16] Because of the biological characteristics of the female, her hygienic needs are greater than the male's hygienic needs. [17] The female on the battle field would not be able to perform as well as the male, because of her monthly cycle and her need for cleanliness and sanitation.

[18] The nurturing role women play in society should not be left invalid, because women are needed in the home to guide and raise their children. [19] Mothering has played a major role in determining women's place in society. [20] In all societies, women are expected to bear children. [21] With women fighting in a war, our population would decline. [22] In addition, women are more patient and understanding than most men. [23] In conclusion, there is no role in society to substitute for a mother. [24] I know that I value and love my mother dearly.

[25] To summerize [sic], women should have equal rights as men because we were all created equal by God. [26] The United States should not [sic] do away with the drafting of women for various reasons. [27] Who will supervise the children at home? [28] Also, women no [sic] that they are not capable of doing physically hard work as men.[1]

Notice that the paper's organization is not arbitrary but designed clearly to display the author's reasoning. Her main arguments are stated in the first paragraph, and then the premises of those arguments, or at least conclusions closely related to them, are supported, in the same order, in the following paragraphs of the paper. Although things go awry in the final paragraph, it was probably meant to recapitulate the main arguments. In this way the student tried to use the structure of the paper as a means of making her reasoning clearer to the reader.

1. This essay was written for "English 9: English Composition: Language as Communication", Section 14, by a George Washington University student in the autumn of 1983. It is used here by kind permission.

II. The first paragraph

Now, let us examine that reasoning, beginning with the first paragraph.

> [1] With the controversy over the proposal for the drafting of women in the armed forces, it is no surprise that there are different opinions from many. [2] However, I feel that women should not be drafted, because they are second class citizens, they are not as physically strong as men, and they play a nurturing role to children.

By means of the illative 'because' the author informs us that she is arguing, that her conclusion is 'Women should not be drafted into the armed forces', and that her premises are 'They [women] are second-class citizens', 'They are not physically as strong as men', and 'They play a nurturing role to children'. Ordinarily, we would put these three premises into a single argument, like this—

> P1. They [women] are second-class citizens.
> P2. They are not physically as strong as men.
> P3. They play a nurturing role to children.
> C. Women should not be drafted into the armed forces.

But the author intends these three premises to support the conclusion independently of each other, and each of them requires the help of different unexpressed premises. So, it will be better to think of them as belonging to three arguments that share the same conclusion:

> A1.
> P. They [women] are second-class citizens.
> C. Women should not be drafted into the armed forces.
> A2.
> P. They are not physically as strong as men.
> C. = A1-C.
> A3.
> P. They play a nurturing role to children.
> C. = A1-C.

What about A1? The Method of Supply allows us to add the unexpressed premise 'No second-class citizens should be drafted into the armed forces', so that the argument that the author probably has in mind is—

A1.

     P1. They [women] are second-class citizens.

   (P2. No second-class citizens should be drafted into the armed forces.)

     C. Women should not be drafted into the armed forces.

Is this argument sound? Although P1 is debatable, P2 more obviously needs support. Here, then, is what we would say to the author: "Your unexpressed premise is that no second-class citizens should be drafted into the armed forces. But this is not self-evidently true. In fact, against it your opponent might plausibly argue that anyone—of whatever class—who enjoys any of the benefits and protections of a society owes it in return his services—including service in the armed forces. So, what can you say in favor of this unexpressed premise?"

Another way of suggesting to the author that the argument, as it stands, is not obviously sound would be to observe that it has applications that she has not anticipated. We would say: "Your argument seems to have some applications that you have not anticipated. If being a second-class citizen is a good reason for exempting women from being drafted into the armed forces, is it an equally good reason for exempting other second-class citizens, such as male minority members? And what about majority males who are not in managerial positions and who earn substantially less money that other males (which seem to be your criteria of first- vs. second-class citizenship)? Are they second-class citizens? Would it be fair to draft them because other males are in such positions? If so, do you assume that it is fair to treat every member of a class the same as every other member of the same class, despite apparently relevant differences between them? But if not, would not that leave us with only comparatively well-paid majority males in managerial positions as subject to the draft? Since they are normally beyond draft age, would there be enough people subject to the draft to serve its military purposes?"[2]

Moreover, the argument's conclusion has a consequence that the author has probably not anticipated. We would say to her: "Your opponent could argue that if women were exempted from the draft, that exemption would be evidence that it would be just to treat them as second-class citizens. For then women, like children, wouldn't shoulder the responsibilities of first-class citizens, so that they, like children, wouldn't deserve to be treated as first-class citizens. How would you answer this objection?"

Now, what about A2? The Method of Supply permits us to add the unexpressed premise 'Men are drafted into the armed forces', so that A2 goes like this:

A2.

     P1. They [women] are not physically as strong as men.

   (P2. Men are drafted into the armed forces.)

     C. Women should not be drafted into the armed forces.

2. An application of an argument is another argument having the same overall form as the original and either some of the same premises or at least other premises of about equal plausibility as the originals.

Is this argument sound or not? Well, to begin with, the student's explicit premise, P1, is so ambiguous that it is hard for us to ascertain whether it is true or false. For it could mean either that no woman is physically as strong as any man (if it means this, it is clearly false) or that the average woman is not physically as strong as the average man (if it means this, it might be true).

In either case, though, P1 is irrelevant to the conclusion, even with the addition of P2. For (a) if it were true that no woman is physically as strong as any man, it would still be as likely as not that some, or even all, women are strong enough to do at least some of the tasks that there are to do in the armed forces. Similarly, (b) even if the average woman is not physically as strong as the average man, it would still be as likely as not that some, or even all, women are strong enough to do at least some of the tasks that there are to do in the armed forces. The only way in which women's strength is relevant to their eligibility for the draft is whether they are strong enough to do what there is to do. Whether they are as strong as men has nothing to do with it.

A2, then, is unsound because it is invalid: its premises make its conclusion neither certain nor probable.

What of A3? The Method of Supply permits us to add an unexpressed premise, so that the author's argument is probably—

A3.
  P1. Women play a nurturing role to children.
  P2. The nurturing role that women play in society should not be left unfilled.
  (P3. A woman cannot both nurture children and serve in the armed forces.)
  C. Women should not be drafted into the armed forces.

P2, which comes from sentence 18, requires support, which the author provides in her fourth paragraph. So we shall postpone discussion of it until then.

Likewise, P3 requires support, so we would say, "Another of your premises is that a woman cannot both nurture children and serve in the armed forces. But your opponent will say that she can do both, either at the same time or at different times. (a) She could do both at the same time if the armed forces made provisions for delivering, housing, feeding, and educating the children of their members. And (b) she could easily do both at different times, since few women bear or care for children continuously throughout their adult lives, and women could be drafted either before or after they bear children. How would you answer your opponent?"

Moreover, the argument's soundness is rendered doubtful by an unanticipated application. We would comment: "Your opponent will say that if your argument is sound when applied to women, it should be equally sound when applied to men. For, unless you absurdly restrict "nurturing" to breast-feeding, men also play a nurturing role to children: they feed them, teach them, and generally bring them up. By parity of reasoning, then, it ought to follow that men, too, should not be drafted. On the other hand, if men's nurturing role toward children is compatible with men's being drafted, why isn't the same true of women? How would you answer your opponent?"

III. The second paragraph

So much for the main arguments, presented in the first paragraph. Now we move on to the second paragraph, which is devoted to supporting the explicit premise ('They [women] are second-class citizens') of A1. In the first sentence of that paragraph ('Women are considered second class citizens, as the role they play in society is inferior to the role men play') the author expresses the argument—

A4.
  P. The role they [women] play in society is inferior to the role men play.
  C. Women are considered second-class citizens.

—, as she tells us by means of the illative 'as'. The conclusion of A4 ('Women are considered second-class citizens') is not quite the same as the explicit premise of A1 ('They [women] are second-class citizens'), since being *considered* a second-class citizen is not the same as *being* one. This makes the relevance of A4 to A1 doubtful, and so we would ask the author to clarify her meaning.

She proceeds in the next two sentences—

[4] For example, men possess the decision-making positions, such as controller over our government and economy. [5] Although women have run for public office, no woman has ever been Vice-President or President; only a few hold positions in our legislature. . . .

—to offer premises to support A4-P. The Aptitude Method tells us that her argument is probably—

A5.
  P1. Men possess the decision-making positions, such as controller over our government and economy.
  P2. No woman has ever been Vice-President or President.
  P3. Only a few women hold positions in our legislatures.
  C. The role they [women] play in society is inferior to the role men play.

The soundness of this argument is compromised by the author's exaggeration in P1 and by her neglect of instances unfavorable to her conclusion. So, we would comment: "Your opponent would say that there are many women in decision-making positions, so that P1

44

is false. And he might say that some states have had female governors. Your conclusion may still be true, but by exaggerating your claim in P1 and omitting any mention of instances not favorable to your case, you stack the evidence in your own favor. How would you respond?"

Furthermore, A5's premises are not relevant to its conclusion. We would say to the author: "Your opponent could claim that, even if it were true that women generally do not play roles requiring the making of consequential decisions, the conclusion still is not even likely, since it is as probable as not that there are some equally important roles (*e.g.,* nurturing children) that they play. So, it is as likely as not that the roles that women play, while different from, are not inferior to, those that men play. You need to answer this."

To make matters worse, A5 has unanticipated applications. We would observe: "What you say of women here is probably true also of professed atheists and communists. Does the same conclusion follow regarding them? Should they too be exempt from the draft, for the same reasons?"

Later in the same paragraph, in sentences 8–10—

[8] Despite the high percentage of working women, few hold executive or managerial positons [*sic*]. [9] A third of working women in the United States hold clerical jobs such as a secretary, a file clerk, and a telephone operator. [10] In general, women receive sixty percent of the pay men receive for the same work. . . .

—, the author presents more premises to support A5-C. Her argument (as the Aptitude Method tells us) is probably—

A6.
   P1. Despite the high percentage of working women, few hold executive or managerial positions.
   P2. A third of working women in the United States hold clerical jobs such as doing secretarial work, filing, and operating telephone switchboards.
   P3. In general, women receive sixty percent of the pay men receive for the same work.
    C. = A5-C = The role they [women] play in society is inferior to the role men play.

The first premise ('Despite the high percentage of working women, few hold executive or managerial positions') is irrelevant to the conclusion that the role women play in society is inferior to the role men play, because, as we would point out to the author, "It does not compare women with men. It is also true that, despite the high percentage of working men, few hold executive or managerial positions. Because of the nature of such positions, there are normally fewer superiors than subordinates, so that there will naturally be fewer men and fewer women in higher than in lower positions. Consequently, this premise doesn't show that women play a lower social role than men, and so it is irrelevant to the conclusion. What you want in its place—provided it is true—is something saying that there are significantly fewer women than men in executive and managerial positions. This would compare women with men in a way that your present premise does not."

Similarly, the second premise is irrelevant to the conclusion. To the author we would say: "That a third of working women in the United States hold clerical jobs such as doing secretarial work, filing, and operating telephone switchboards is irrelevant to the conclusion that the role women play in society is inferior to the role men play, because it doesn't compare women with men. It could be that a third of working men in the United States hold comparably menial jobs, such as collecting garbage, digging ditches, or moving furniture, so that women and men play equally low social roles. To support the conclusion, you need a premise that would say that there are significantly more women than men in menial or undesirable jobs."

Concerning P3, we would say: "Your third premise is relevant to the conclusion, regardless of the reason why women are paid significantly less than men for the same work. This is the best part of A6."

Sentences 6–7—

[6] If women are drafted, our society will have to be more lenient towards women, by giving them more authority and power in the decision-making of our government. [7] As the Equal Rights for Women has not been ratified in all states, women should refuse to register for the draft. . . .

—and 11—

[11] With the ratification of the Equal Rights Amendment for women, Congress would have no alternative but to grant women the same pay as men for the same work. . . .

—are irrelevant to the conclusion of the paragraph. They interrupt and distract attention from the author's argument, so they should be omitted from this paragraph.

IV. The third paragraph

That brings us to the third paragraph. The opening sentence—

[12] The female's physical characteristics are different from the male's physical characteristics as the female body is structured differently. . . .

—expresses the argument—

A7.
>   P. The female body is structured differently [from the male].
>   C. The female's physical characteristics are different from the male's physical characteristics.

—, as the illative 'as' reveals. But, for all this argument tells us, the female's body might be stronger than the male's; for it draws, between the female and male physical structures and characteristics, only the vague comparison that they are "different." There are various ways in which they might be "different": the male's body might be stronger than the female's, the female's might be stronger than the male's, the male's might be taller, or fatter, and so on. A more precise comparison is needed to support the main conclusion of the essay, that women should not be drafted into the armed forces.

The third paragraph's second sentence is: 'The female body is not structured to render physically demanding work.' The Aptitude Method and the Method of Supply allow us to conclude that the author's argument is probably—

A8.
>   P1. The female body is not structured to render physically demanding work.
>   (P2. The male body is structured to render physically demanding work.)
>   C. The female body is structured differently [from the male body].

Now, the explicit premise of this argument is false. So, we would say to the author: "This premise is contradicted by the fact that some women perform physically demanding work—*e.g.,* athletics, farming, delivering packages, construction work. And don't forget that there are female bodybuilders who develop considerable strength through 'physically demanding work.' "

The next sentence ('Being drafted in the military, women would not be able to perform some of the tasks men perform because women are usually less powerful and smaller') expresses the argument—

A9.
>   P. Women are usually less powerful and smaller [than men].
>   C. Being drafted in the military, women would not be able to perform some of the tasks men perform.

Although we might expect the conclusion of this argument to be meant to support A2-P1 ('They [women] are not physically as strong as men'), it probably is not. For A9-C would not plausibly be a reason for A2-P1. In fact, that the author believes that the reverse is true is proved by the fact that she offers A9-P (which says all that A2-P1 says, and then some) as a reason for A9-C. So, what further conclusion is A9-C intended to support? Probably the main conclusion of the essay, giving us the argument—

A10.
P1. = A9-C = Being drafted in the military, women would not be able to perform some of the tasks men perform.
(P2. Every woman who is drafted into the armed forces should be able to perform all the same tasks as every man who is drafted.)
C. Women should not be drafted into the armed forces.

If this is the argument-chain the author has in mind, her unexpressed premise in A10 requires support. We would say to her: "In order to get from the premise 'Being drafted in the military, women would not be able to perform some of the tasks men perform' to the conclusion 'Women shouldn't be drafted into the armed forces', you must assume the premise 'Every woman who is drafted into the armed forces should be able to perform all the same tasks as every man who is drafted'. Without that premise, the conclusion will not follow. Yet that premise is not obviously true, and in fact it is probably false. For the same thing doesn't hold true even of men who are drafted: some men who are drafted are unable to perform all the same tasks as every other man who is drafted. So, why should it be true of women when it is not true of men?"

Next is sentence 15: 'Furthermore, women are known to be more emotional then [sic] men because women panic easily.' This clearly has nothing to do with the main conclusion of the paragraph—namely, that women are not physically as strong as men. It seems instead to be part of an independent argument-chain for the main conclusion of the essay:

A11.
P1. Women panic easily.
(P2. Men do not panic easily.)
(P3. Of two people, if one panics more easily than the other, he is the more emotional.)
C. Women are more emotional than men.
A12.
P1. = A11-C.
(P2. Whoever is more emotional than men should not be drafted into the armed forces.)
C. Women should not be drafted into the armed forces.

A11-P1 and -P2 are ambiguous. We would comment to the author: "You say that women panic easily, and you assume that men do not panic easily. But both of these premises are ambiguous. They could mean either that all, that most, or that only some women or men do or do not panic easily. And, naturally, not only whether these premises are true or false but also whether they support the conclusion depend on exactly what they say. What, then, do you mean?"

Another problem with A11 is that A11-P3 is not true. To the author we would say: "You take for granted the premise that, of two people, if one panics more easily than the other, he is the more emotional; only by assuming this premise can you reach the conclusion that women are more emotional than men. But panic is not the only kind of emotion: there are many other kinds. Therefore, someone who panics easily may still not be as emotional as someone who does not, provided the second person is enough more emotional in other ways. For instance, the second person might be much more aggressive and greedy than the first and so, on the whole, more emotional. The only way you could save this premise would be to revise it to say that, other things being equal, he who panics more easily is more emotional. But that wouldn't improve the argument, since we can't keep other things equal: everything must be taken into consideration when we inquire whether women are more emotional than men."

That brings us to the final part of the third paragraph, sentences 16 and 17:

[16] Because of the biological characteristics of the female, her hygienic needs are greater than the male's hygienic needs. [17] The female on the battle field would not be able to perform as well as the male, because of her monthly cycle and her need for cleanliness and sanitation.

This part of the paragraph, too, seems to be devoted to supporting, not A2-P1 ('They [women] are not physically as strong as men'), but the essay's main conclusion, 'Women should not be drafted into the armed forces'. The author's argument-chain seems to be:

A13.
    P. The female has certain biological characteristics—namely, her monthly cycle and her need for cleanliness and sanitation.
    C. Her hygienic needs are greater than the male's.
A14.
    P. = A13-C.
    C. The female on the battlefield would not be able to perform as well as the male.
A15.
    P. = A14-C.
    C. Women should not be drafted into the armed forces.

A14 is invalid. For it is deductive (by default), but its premise does not make its conclusion certain. To the author we would say: "Whether the female's greater hygienic needs would make her less competent on the battlefield depends on the degree to which those needs, and their satisfaction, would interfere with her performance in battle. Until that is specified, in a premise, the conclusion will not follow."

Similarly, A15 is invalid. For it too is deductive (by default), but its premise does not make its conclusion certain. We would say: "Even if it were true that the female would not be able to perform as well as the male on the battlefield, it still would not follow that women should not be drafted. For even if during their menstrual periods they couldn't perform as well as men on the battlefield, (a) they might still perform well enough to make it worthwhile having them there; (b) they might be reserved from battle only during their menstrual periods; and (c) they might be assigned support, rather than battlefield, duty."

V. The fourth paragraph

We are now at the fourth paragraph. Its first sentence is: 'The nurturing role women play in society should not be left invalid, because women are needed in the home to guide and raise their children.' As the illative 'because' tells us, this sentence expresses the argument—

A16.
P. Women are needed in the home to guide and raise their children.
C. The nurturing role women play in society should not be left unfilled ("invalid").

The soundness of this argument is made doubtful by an unanticipated application. We would comment: "Your opponent will say that your argument applies as well to men as to women: they, too, are needed in the home to guide and raise their children; therefore, their nurturing role should not be left unfilled. Do you accept the implicit consequence that neither men nor women should be drafted? If not, why do you think the argument works when applied to women but not when applied to men?"

The next sentence is: 'Mothering has played a major role in determining women's place in society.' In this and the preceding sentence the Aptitude Method permits us to detect the argument—

A17.
P. Mothering has played a major role in determining women's place in society.
C. The nurturing role women play in society should not be left unfilled ("invalid").

But this argument is invalid. We would comment: "Given that mothering has played a major role in determining women's place in society, it does not follow that women should continue to play their nurturing role in society. For (a) if, as you said in sentences 2–3, women play the inferior social role of second-class citizens; and if mothering has in large part determined women's place in society; perhaps mothering is keeping them down, and it would be better for women if they abandoned, or at least shared with men, their nurturing role. (b) As long as mothering has only played a "major", and not an "exclusive", role in determining women's place in society, it remains possible that other things besides mothering (*e.g.,* tolerating second-class citizenship, being smaller and weaker than men, or even defending their country) have determined women's place in society, so that it mightn't be so bad if their nurturing role were left unfilled. (c) There may be a pressing need for women temporarily to abandon their traditional roles and serve in the military."

Sentences 21–24 are:

[21] With women fighting in a war, our population would decline. [22] In addition, women are more patient and understanding than most men. [23] In conclusion, there is no role in society to substitute for a mother. [24] I know that I value and love my mother dearly.

The author may have in mind this argument:

A18.
    P1. With women fighting in a war, our population would decline.
    P2. Women are more patient and understanding than most men.
    P3. I know that I value and love my mother dearly.
    C. There is no role in society to substitute for a mother.

If so, it is pretty obviously invalid. Moreover, the relevance of P1 and P3 to the conclusion is made questionable by an unanticipated application. We would comment: "This part of the argument applies to men as well as women, in the following way:

A19.
    P1. With men fighting in a war, our population would decline.
    P2. I know that I value and love my father dearly.
    C. There is no role in society to substitute for a father.

Does this application help to show that men should not be drafted but should instead stay at home, fathering children? If not, why do you think that this part of the argument works in the case of women but not men?"

CHAPTER NINE

CONCLUDING ADVICE TO STUDENTS

Now that you know a little about logic, we can give you the following advice on the reasoning you express in your writing.

1. Express your arguments clearly and without ambiguity. Your reader shouldn't have to guess what you mean.

2. Maintain a consistent position. Keep it free of internal contradictions.

3. Don't merely state and repeat, but offer good arguments for, your position. In particular:

    a. Be aware of your unexpressed premises, even though you don't state them for your reader.

    b. Are any of your premises—whether expressed or not—false? If so, discard them. Are any improbable or disputable? If so, defend them. That is, make them the conclusions of other arguments.

    c. Are your premises the *best* evidence you might have used to support your conclusion? If not, your reader will wonder why you are using inferior evidence.

    d. Do your premises or conclusion have any false, improbable, disputable, or otherwise unacceptable presuppositions or consequences? If so, reconsider them.

    e. Do any of your arguments have unacceptable applications to different subject-matter? If so, reconsider them.

    f. Do any of your premises presuppose your conclusion? If so, your argument begs the question—*i.e.*, it takes for granted the very thing it is supposed to prove.

    g. Are your arguments valid? That is, if you claim that the premises make the conclusion certain, *do* they? Would the falsity of your conclusion be inconsistent with the truth of all your premises? And if you claim that the premises make the conclusion only probable, *do* they? Are the premises at least relevant to the conclusion? Could a competing conclusion be drawn from the same premises?

4. Anticipate and answer the most serious objections to your premises and conclusion.

5. Refute the strongest arguments in favor of the other side.

6. Above all: if the balance of the evidence is against you, change your mind.

WORKBOOK

INSTRUCTIONS

This workbook is not designed to be read page-by-page, like an ordinary book. So, don't try to read it that way. Instead, when you are assigned an exercise set, look it up in the table of contents and turn to the page listed. There you will find the first question, followed by five possible answers. Read the question and answers carefully and decide which answer you think is *best*. Write down the letter corresponding to that answer on the answer sheet you will hand in later. Then—and *only* then—turn to the page whose number is given immediately after that answer. When you reach that page, find the commentary to that answer and read it. If your answer was correct, the commentary will tell you so and send you on to the next question. If it was incorrect, the commentary will tell you why and send you back to the same question for another try. If you chose answer (a), (b), or (c), and it was incorrect, then on your answer sheet explain in your own words what was wrong with your answer. If you chose (d) or (e), and it was incorrect, you can omit the written explanation. Then return to the question and try again. Follow the same procedures for all questions. Page numbers will always be provided to tell you where to go next. And in case you get lost, in the back of the book there is an index that gives the page number of each question and commentary. When you are finished, you should have an answer sheet, complete with corrections, ready to hand in.

5.10 Question

Text:

> Phillips' [Dr. Ian Phillips of London's St. Thomas's Hospital] find [namely, a strain of gonococci that are resistant to penicillin] was not unique. The new strain of bacteria had shown up in several other laboratories in Britain, and doctors at Travis Air Force Base in California encountered penicillin-proof gonococci in a young Air Force noncom who had just returned from the Philippines. Another example was reported in Maryland. By last week Atlanta's Center for Disease Control had verified 33 cases of gonorrhea in the U.S. that did not respond to conventional penicillin therapy. . . .

> —"The Penicillin Eaters", *Time,* Vol. 108, No. 21 (November 22, 1976), p. 53. (Tim Kuck)

Analysis:

P1. The new strain of bacteria had shown up in several other laboratories in Britain.

P2. Doctors at Travis Air Force Base in California encountered penicillin-proof gonococci in a young Air Force noncom who had just returned from the Philippines.

P3. Another example was reported in Maryland.

P4. By last week Atlanta's Center for Disease Control had verified 33 cases of gonorrhea in the U.S. that did not respond to conventional penicillin therapy.

C. Phillips' find [namely, a strain of gonococci that are resistant to penicillin] was not unique.

Which of the following answers is best?

a. The argument is deductive, because the conclusion says that Phillips' find definitely was *not* unique. (Page 152)

b. The premises jointly do not make the conclusion certain. (Page 164)

c. The argument is valid and inductive. (Page 138)

d. More than one of the above answers are correct. (Page 92)

e. Answers (a) through (d) are all incorrect. (Page 174)

Either you're browsing or you've made a mistake and should go back where you came from. Remember that this is a programmed workbook and so should not be read as if it were an ordinary book. There are instructions with each question telling you to which page you should turn next.

is— This is the best answer, as (a), (b), and (c) are all correct. The first part of the text

And because the condition of man, as hath been declared in the precedent chapter, is a condition of war of every one against every one; in which case every one is governed by his own reason; and there is nothing he can make use of, that may not be a help to him, in preserving his life against his enemies; it followeth, that in such a condition, every man has a right to every thing; even to one another's body. . . .

—, in which the illatives 'because' and 'it followeth that' work together to indicate the argument analyzed in answer (a):

A1.
P1. The condition of man is a condition of war of every one against every one.
P2. In this case every one is governed by his own reason.
P3. There is nothing he can make use of, that may not be a help to him, in preserving his life against his enemies.
C. In such a condition, every man has a right to every thing; even to one another's body.

The next, overlapping part of the text is—

. . . in such a condition, every man has a right to every thing; even to one another's body. And therefore, as long as this natural right of every man to every thing endureth, there can be no security to any man, how strong or wise soever he be, of living out the time, which nature ordinarily alloweth men to live. . . .

—, in which the illative 'therefore' indicates the argument analyzed in answer (b):

A2.
P. = A1-C.
C. As long as this natural right of every man to every thing endureth, there can be no security to any man, how strong or wise soever he be, of living out the time, which nature ordinarily alloweth men to live.

And the next, overlapping part of the text is—

> . . . as long as this natural right of every man to every thing endureth, there can be no security to any man, how strong or wise soever he be, of living out the time, which nature ordinarily alloweth men to live. And consequently it is a precept, or a general rule of reason, *that every man, ought to endeavour peace, as far as he has hope of obtaining it; and when he cannot obtain it, that he may seek, and use, all helps, and advantages of war.* . . .

—, in which the illative 'consequently' indicates the argument analyzed in answer (c):

A3.
    P. = A2-C.
    C. It is a precept, or a general rule of reason, *that every man, ought to endeavor peace, as far as he has hope of obtaining it; and when he cannot obtain it, that he may seek, and use, all helps and advantages of war.*

The final part of the text—

> The first branch of which rule, containeth the first, and fundamental law of nature; which is, *to seek peace, and follow it.* The second, the sum of the right of nature; which is, *by all means we can, to defend ourselves.*

—is extraneous to the arguments that the text expresses.

This text thus expresses a three-argument chain. The text may at first have looked forbidding because of its length, its archaic language, and its subject matter; but the analysis of its arguments has turned out to be easy, thanks to its illatives.

The next question is on page 134.

5.1 Answer (e)

This answer is correct, because all the others are wrong. An arguer thinks that his premises make his conclusion probable or certain. His argument is valid if, and only if, its premises actually do what he thinks they do. That is, if he thinks they make the conclusion probable, then the argument is valid if they actually do make the conclusion probable; and if the arguer thinks the premises make the conclusion certain, then the argument is valid if they actually do so. For instance, the text—

> Most stonemasons are right-handed, and Socrates is a stonemason. From this it follows that Socrates is right-handed.

—expresses the argument—

> P1. Most stonemasons are right-handed.
> P2. Socrates is a stonemason.
> C. Socrates is right-handed.

This argument is invalid, since (1) the author believes his premises make his conclusion certain, as his use of the illative 'From this it follows that' shows; but (2) the premises actually make the conclusion not certain but only probable. Similarly, the text—

> Three is greater than two, and two is greater than one. In view of this, it is likely that three is greater than one.

—expresses the argument—

> P1. Three is greater than two.
> P2. Two is greater than one.
> C. Three is greater than one.

This argument is also invalid, because (1) the author believes that his premises make his conclusion probable, as his use of the illative 'In view of this, it is likely that' shows; but (2) his premises actually make the conclusion not probable but certain. Answers (a), (b), and (c) all leave the arguer's beliefs out of account, and that is why they (and consequently (d) as well) are wrong.

Proceed to the next question, on page 122.

4.8 Answer (d)

No more than one of the answers (a) through (c) are correct, so that (d) is incorrect. Return to page 117 to try again.

1.2 *Answer (e)*

At least one of the answers (a) through (d) is correct, so that (e) is incorrect. Return to page 129 to try again.

2.3 *Answer (e)*

At least one of the answers (a) through (d) is correct, so that (e) is incorrect. Return to page 118 to try again.

3.4 *Answer (e)*

At least one of the answers (a) through (d) is correct, so that (e) is incorrect. Return to page 109 to try again.

4.1 *Answer (e)*

At least one of the answers (a) through (d) is correct, so that (e) is incorrect. Return to page 94 to try again.

5.7 *Answer (d)*

No more than one of the answers (a) through (c) are correct, so that (d) is incorrect. Return to page 103 to try again.

6.3 *Answer (d)*

No more than one of the answers (a) through (c) are correct, so that (d) is incorrect. Return to page 138 to try again.

5.6 Question

Text:

> What is it then in this bit of wax that we recognize with so much distinctness [after the wax has been brought near the fire]? Certainly it cannot be anything that I observe by means of the senses, since everything in the field of taste, smell, sight, touch, and hearing are [*sic*] changed, and since the wax nevertheless remains.

> —René Descartes, *Meditations on First Philosophy* (1641), tr. Laurence J. Lafleur (Indianapolis: The Bobbs-Merrill Company, Inc., 1960), II, p. 29.

Analysis:

P1. Everything in this bit of wax in the field of taste, smell, sight, touch, and hearing is changed.

P2. The same wax nevertheless remains.

C. That which, in this bit of wax, we recognize [as the same after the wax has been brought near the fire] cannot be anything I [René Descartes] observed by means of the (five) senses.

Which of the following answers is best?

a. This text expresses an invalid deductive argument. (Page 157)

b. This text expresses a valid inductive argument. (Page 170)

c. This text expresses a valid deductive argument. (Page 126)

d. More than one of the above answers are correct. (Page 146)

e. Answers (a) through (d) are all incorrect. (Page 99)

6.2 Answer (d)

This is the best answer, as answers (a) and (c) are both correct. For further details, see the commentaries to those answers, on pages 101 and 163.

The next question is on page 138.

2.5 Answer (b)

This answer is incorrect. The argument that the text expresses is:

> P1. A thought is a sentence.
> P2. A sentence is a picture.
> C. A thought is a picture.

(For details, see the commentary to answer (a).) As it stands, this argument does not *need* another premise: the two it has are sufficient to make the conclusion certain, which (as the hint provided with the question says) is probably what the author had in mind. As it stands, then, the argument is not defective and so does not need an additional premise. Consequently, answer (b) is wrong.

After writing a brief explanation why this answer is incorrect, return to page 97 for another try.

4.3 Question

Text:

> It is beyond all question that the action of music was far more direct in the case of ancient races than it is with us, because mankind is much more easily impressed by elemental forces in a primitive state of culture than later on, when intellectual consciousness and the faculty of reflection have attained a higher degree of maturity. . . .

—Eduard Hanslick, *The Beautiful in Music* (1854; 7th Edition, 1885), tr. Gustav Cohen (1891), ed. Morris Weitz (Indianapolis: The Bobbs-Merrill Company, Inc., 1957), Ch. 5, p. 95.

This text expresses the argument—

P. Mankind is much more easily impressed by elemental forces in a primitive state of culture than later on, when intellectual consciousness and the faculty of reflection have attained a higher degree of maturity.

C. The action of music was far more direct in the case of ancient races than it is with us.

That this argument is deductive, we properly discover by considering the fact(s) that:

a. The expression 'It is beyond all question that' tells us that the author believes that the proposition 'The action of music was far more direct in the case of ancient races than it is with us' is certain. (Page 147)

b. The illative 'because' tells us that the author thinks that the premise makes the conclusion certain. (Page 132)

c. The author uses no expression that tells us whether he thinks the premise makes the conclusion probable or certain. Consequently, we assume that he thinks his premise makes the conclusion certain. (Page 169)

d. More than one of the above answers are correct. (Page 99)

e. Answers (a) through (d) are all incorrect. (Page 120)

5.2 Answer (a)

This answer is incorrect: it is false that an argument is sound if and only if it contains no false premise. For (1) it is false that an argument is sound *if* it contains no false premise, and (2) it is false that an argument is sound *only if* it contains no false premise.

Proof of (1): an argument can be unsound although all its premises are true. For instance, if someone says—

Since three is greater than two, and since two is greater than one, it follows that nine is the square of three.

—, his argument—

P1. Three is greater than two.
P2. Two is greater than one.
C. Nine is the square of three.

—would be unsound, although it contains no false premise.

Proof of (2): an argument can be sound although some of its premises are false. For instance, if someone says—

If my grandmother were a trolley, and if all trolleys had wheels, my grandmother certainly would have wheels.

—, his argument—

> P1. My grandmother were a trolley.
> P2. All trolleys had wheels.
> C. My grandmother would have wheels.

—would be sound, although at least its first premise is false. Hence, it is false that an argument is sound only if it contains no false premise.

Return to page 122 to try again.

1.10 Question

Text:

> Indians are very big nowadays; nevertheless one did not expect the contemporary fascination with the first Americans to bring back any of the music on Indian themes produced in response to the short-lived musical nationalism of the 1890's. [Edward] MacDowell's *Indian* Suite is probably the best work that movement produced; it is also, in all probability, MacDowell's finest work for orchestra alone.

—Alfred Frankenstein, review of Turnabout album TV–S34535, *High Fidelity,* Vol. 24, No. 4 (April 1974), p. 98.

Which of the following answers is best?

a. The illative 'nevertheless' here indicates this argument:

> P. Indians are very big nowadays.
> C. One did not expect the contemporary fascination with the first Americans to bring back any of the music on Indian themes produced in response to the short-lived musical nationalism of the 1890's.

(Page 139)

b. The illative 'probably' here indicates this argument:

P. Edward MacDowell's *Indian* Suite is, in all probability, his finest work for orchestra alone.
C. Edward MacDowell's *Indian* Suite is the best work produced by the short-lived musical nationalism of the 1890's.

(Page 84)

c. The illative 'in all probability' here indicates this argument:

P. Edward MacDowell's *Indian* Suite is probably the best work produced by the short-lived musical nationalism of the 1890's.
C. Edward MacDowell's *Indian* Suite is his finest work for orchestra alone.

(Page 169)

d. More than one of the above answers are correct. (Page 146)

e. Answers (a) through (d) are all incorrect. (Page 96)

1.4 Answer (c)

This answer is incorrect, because it is *only sometimes* true that an illative comes after a conclusion but before a premise. The illative 'for', for instance, in the text—

Socrates is mortal; for he is a man, and all men are mortal.

—, follows a conclusion and precedes a premise. But illatives like 'therefore', 'so', and 'hence' ordinarily follow a premise rather than a conclusion and precede a conclusion rather than a premise. For instance, in the text—

All men are mortal, and Socrates is a man. So, Socrates is mortal.

—, the illative 'so' follows the premise 'Socrates is a man' and precedes the conclusion 'Socrates is mortal'. Moreover, some illatives, like 'since' and 'because', although they ordinarily precede a premise, sometimes do and sometimes do not follow a conclusion. For instance, in the text—

Socrates is mortal, since he is a man, and all men are mortal.

—, the illative 'since' comes after the conclusion 'Socrates is mortal' and before the premise 'He is a man'; but in the text—

Since all men are mortal, and Socrates is a man, he is mortal.

—, 'since' does not come after a conclusion, although it does still precede a premise. So, it is not true that an illative always comes after a conclusion but before a premise.

After writing on your answer sheet a brief explanation why this answer is wrong, return to page 121 to try again.

1.7 Question

Text:

> Furthermore, this fact that the material is indifferent to the division of time leads to the conclusion that the lapse of time is an accident, rather than of the essence, of the material. . . .

—Alfred North Whitehead, *Science and the Modern World* (New York: The Free Press, 1925, 1953), p. 50.

This text is admittedly obscure. But if you learned what Chapter One taught about illatives, you should be able to understand enough of the text to say which of the following answers is best.

a. The illative 'Furthermore' tells us that this text expresses the argument—

P. This fact that the material is indifferent to the division of time.
C. The lapse of time is an accident, rather than of the essence, of the material.

(Page 140)

b. The illative 'this fact that . . . leads to the conclusion that' tells us that this text expresses the argument—

P. The lapse of time is an accident, rather than of the essence, of the material.

C. The material is indifferent to the division of time.

(Page 94)

    c. There is no illative in this text, so that we must rely on the Aptitude Method to ascertain whether the text expresses an argument. (Page 124)

    d. More than one of the above answers are correct. (Page 174)

    e. Answers (a) through (d) are all incorrect. (Page 162)

1.11 Answer (e)

At least one of the answers (a) through (d) is correct, so that (e) is incorrect. Return to page 90 to try again.

4.5 Answer (d)

No more than one of the answers (a) through (c) are correct, so that (d) is incorrect. Return to page 105 to try again.

5.8 Answer (d)

There you go! Answers (a), (b), and (c) are all correct. The argument is deductive, as 'this shews that' and 'must' indicate; but its premise does not render its conclusion certain; and so the argument is invalid.

Proceed to page 74 for the next question.

6.8 Answer (c)

This answer is correct. But is it the only correct one? Return to page 110 to try again.

2.1 Answer (b)

This answer is incorrect, since it is not true that any unexpressed premise that we add to our analysis of an argument should plausibly assist any expressed premises to make the conclusion *certain*. For the author may not have intended his premises to make his conclusion certain. For example, the author if the text—

Socrates is probably right-handed, as he is a stonemason.

—thinks that his premises make his conclusion, 'Socrates is right-handed', not certain but only probable, as his use of the word 'probably' tells us. Consequently, we would not be completing the argument that the author had in mind if we were to add an unexpressed premise that, like 'All stonemasons are right-handed', would help the expressed premise to make the conclusion not probable but certain.

After writing on your answer sheet a brief explanation why this answer is wrong, return to page 160 to try again.

3.7 Question

Text:

And because the condition of man, as hath been declared in the precedent chapter, is a condition of war of every one against every one; in which case every one is governed by his own reason; and there is nothing he can make use of, that may not be a help to him, in preserving his life against his enemies; it followeth that in such a condition, every man has a right to every thing; even to one another's body. And therefore, as long as this natural right of every man to every thing endureth, there can be no security to any man, how strong or wise soever he be, of living out the time, which nature ordinarily alloweth men to live. And consequently it is a precept, or a general rule of reason, *that every man, ought to endeavour peace, as far as he has hope of obtaining it; and when he cannot obtain it, that he may seek, and use, all helps, and advantages of war.* The first branch of which rule, containeth the first, and fundamental law of nature; which is, *to seek peace, and follow it.* The second, the sum of the right of nature; which is, *by all means we can, to defend ourselves.*

—Thomas Hobbes, *Leviathan: or the Matter, Forme and Power of a Commonwealth Ecclesiasticall and Civil* (1651); ed. Michael Oakeshott (New York: Collier Books, 1962), I, 14; pp. 103–104.

Don't be intimidated by the apparent difficulty of this text; for if you attend to its illatives, you can ascertain which of the following answers is best.

a. This text expresses the argument—

P1. The condition of man is a condition of war of every one against every one.
P2. In this case every one is governed by his own reason.
P3. There is nothing he can make use of, that may not be a help to him, in preserving his life against his enemies.
C. In such a condition, every man has a right to every thing; even to one another's body.

(Page 128)

b. This text expresses the argument—

P. In a condition of war of every man against every other man, every man has a right to every thing; even to one another's body.
C. As long as this natural right of every man to every thing endureth, there can be no security to any man, how strong or wise soever he be, of living out the time, which nature ordinarily alloweth men to live.

(Page 92)

c. This text expresses the argument—

P. As long as this natural right of every man to every thing endureth, there can be no security to any man, how strong or wise soever he be, of living out the time, which nature ordinarily alloweth men to live.
C. It is a precept, or a general rule of reason, *that every man, ought to endeavor peace, as far as he has hope of attaining it; and when he cannot obtain it, that he may seek, and use, all helps and advantages of war.*

(Page 113)

d. More than one of the above answers are correct. (Page 61)

e. Answers (a) through (d) are all incorrect. (Page 138)

3.5 Answer (c)

It is true that the text expresses an argument in which 'No one would choose the whole world on condition of being alone' is a conclusion: the illative 'since' tells us so. Hence, answer (c) is correct. But is it the only correct answer?

Return to page 122 to reconsider the question.

4.7 Answer (d)

No more than one of the answers (a) through (c) are correct, so that (d) is incorrect. Return to page 89 to try again.

5.9 Question

Text:

> But once they get there [IHS hospitals or clinics], Indians are more likely than not to enter inadequate facilities. . . . A two-year study of IHS found that only 22 of its 51 hospitals meet minimum accreditation standards, that only 16 of them meet national fire and safety codes, that 19 should be replaced and 14 extensively modernized at a cost of $200 million. . . .

> —"Troublesome Implications", *The Wall Street Journal,* Vol. CLXXXIV, No. 60 (September 30, 1974), p. 14, col. 1. (Diane Berthelsen)

Analysis:

P1. A two-year study of IHS found that only 22 of its 51 hospitals meet minimum accreditation standards, that only 16 of them meet national fire and safety codes, and that 19 should be replaced and 14 extensively modernized at a cost of $200 million.

(P2. Hospitals that fail to meet national fire and safety codes or that should be replaced or extensively modernized are inadequate facilities.)

C. Once they get there [IHS hospitals or clinics], Indians enter inadequate facilities.

Which of the following answers is best?

a. The argument is deductive, as the expression 'more than likely' tells us. (Page 144)

b. The argument is valid and inductive. (Page 91)

c. The premise is logically irrelevant to the conclusion. (Page 172)

d. More than one of the above answers are correct. (Page 160)

e. Answers (a) through (d) are all incorrect. (Page 116)

5.5 Question

Which of the following answers is best?

a. The author of the following text has in mind a sound argument:

> In view of the fact that Alabama is entirely east of Mississippi, it is also entirely east of Tennessee.

(Page 140)

b. The author of the following text has in mind a sound argument:

> If Hawaii were Wyoming, it would have no coastline.

(Page 151)

c. The author of the following text has in mind a sound argument:

> Since Louisiana is south of Arkansas, it is also south of Missouri.

(Page 161)

d. More than one of the above answers are correct. (Page 128)

e. Answers (a) through (d) are all incorrect. (Page 113)

1.5 *Answer (e)*

At least one of the answers (a) through (d) is correct, so that (e) is incorrect.
Return to page 87 to try again.

2.2 *Answer (e)*

At least one of the answers (a) through (d) is correct, so that (e) is incorrect.
Return to page 135 to try again.

3.8 *Answer (d)*

No more than one of the answers (a) through (c) are correct, so that (d) is incorrect.
Return to page 134 to try again.

5.7 *Answer (a)*

This answer is incorrect, because the argument is not valid.
Return to page 103 to try again.

6.4 Question

Which of the following answers is best?

   a. An author's use of any of the following illatives would tell us that his argument is verificatory:

     i. . . . is evidence for . . .
     ii. . . . confirms my suspicion that . . .
     iii. Therefore

(Page 141)

b. An author's use of any of the following illatives would tell us that his argument is explanatory:

  i. Because
  ii. . . . is due to . . .
  iii. . . . produced the result that . . .

(Page 111)

c. An author's use of any of the following illatives would *not* tell us whether his argument is verificatory or explanatory:

  i. Since
  ii. So
  iii. For

(Page 128)

d. More than one of the above answers are correct. (Page 156)

e. Answers (a) through (d) are all incorrect. (Page 99)

2.4 Answer (c)

Answer (c) says that the proposition 'Their own written records are one way we have of knowing about the origins of a people' should be added to the argument as an unexpressed premise. Let us see why this is incorrect.

The text contains the illative ':', which means that it expresses the argument—

P. The Moors were ignorant of the use of letters.
C. The origin of the Moors is involved [*i.e.,* enveloped, shrouded] in darkness.

(For further remarks on the analysis of this argument, see the commentary to answer (a).) And the hint provided with the question advises you, in the absence of evidence to the contrary, to assume that the author thinks that his premises make his conclusion certain. Therefore, if this argument were not to be defective, its one premise would have to make its conclusion certain—which it obviously does not do. For the premise talks about *being ignorant of the use of letters,* while the conclusion talks about *having origins that are enveloped in darkness,* and the argument provides no connection between these two concepts. So, the argument is defective and needs at least one unexpressed premise to make the needed connection, so that the premises will make the conclusion certain.

Now, answer (c) suggests that 'Their own written records are one way we have of knowing about the origins of a people' be added as an unexpressed premise. But this won't do, since it would not help the expressed premise to make the conclusion *certain;* for the propositions that the Moors were ignorant of the use of letters, and that their own written records are one way we have of knowing about the origins of a people, are jointly compatible with the falsity of the conclusion—*i.e.,* together they are consistent with the origin of the Moors *not* being involved in darkness. For instance, it would still be possible that we have ways, other than consulting their written records, of learning about the origins of a people; in which case the origin of the Moors would not be involved in darkness. Answer (c), then, is wrong, because 'Their own written records are one way we have of knowing about the origin of a people' would not plausibly be a reason for the conclusion— at least, not the kind of reason the author has in mind—namely, the kind of reason that would help to make the conclusion certain.

After writing on your answer sheet a brief explanation why this answer is wrong, return to page 91 to try again.

1.8 Question

Text:

> Since the One is the source of all things and includes all things in it, it cannot be defined in terms of those things, since no matter what thing you use to define it, the thing will always describe something less than the One itself. . . .

> —Robert M. Pirsig, *Zen and the Art of Motorcycle Maintenance* (Toronto: Bantam Books, 1974), p. 381.

Again, you don't have to understand everything in this text in order to be able to ascertain which of the following answers is best.

    a. This text expresses two arguments, each indicated by an occurrence of the illative 'since':

      First argument
      P. The One is the source of all things and includes all things in it.
      C. The One cannot be defined in terms of those things.

Second argument

P. No matter what thing you use to define the One, the thing will always describe something less than the One itself.

C. The One cannot be defined in terms of those things.

(Page 166)

b. This text expresses the argument—

P1. The One is the source of all things and includes all things in it.

P2. No matter what thing you use to define it [*i.e.,* the One], the thing will always describe something less than the One itself.

C. It [the One] cannot be defined in terms of those things.

—, whose first premise and conclusion are indicated by the first occurrence of the illative 'since' and whose second premise and conclusion are indicated by the second occurrence of 'since'. (Page 145)

c. This text expresses the argument—

P. [It is] no matter what thing you use to define the One.

C. The thing will always describe something less than the One itself.

(Page 173)

d. More than one of the above answers are correct. (Page 92)

e. Answers (a) through (d) are all incorrect. (Page 156)

5.1 Answer (c)

This answer may look good in comparison with (a) and (b), but unfortunately it is incorrect, too. For instance, the text—

Most stonemasons are right-handed, and Socrates is a stonemason. From this it follows that Socrates is right-handed.

—expresses the argument—

P1. Most stonemasons are right-handed.
P2. Socrates is a stonemason.
C. Socrates is right-handed.

This argument conforms to the description in answer (c). For its premises actually make its conclusion *either probable or certain,* since they make it probable. And yet the argument is invalid. Similarly, the text—

> Three is greater than two, and two is greater than one. In view of this, it is likely that three is greater than one.

—expresses the argument—

P1. Three is greater than two.
P2. Two is greater than one.
C. Three is greater than one.

This argument also conforms to the description in answer (c): its premises actually make its conclusion *either probable or certain,* inasmuch as they make it certain. And yet this argument is also invalid. As these two examples show, an argument may conform to the description in answer (c) and yet not be valid, so that answer (c) is incorrect.

Return to page 168 to try again.

1.12 Question

Text:

> I have consulted few specialist studies during the actual writing of this book. I wished to write directly from the texts [of the early Greek philosophers] themselves, and with the student, not the scholar, in mind. . . .

—John Mansley Robinson, *An Introduction to Early Greek Philosophy* (Boston: Houghton Mifflin Co., 1968), p. viii. (Mike Stonefield)

This text expresses:

a. The argument—

P. I [John Mansley Robinson] have consulted few specialist studies during the actual writing of this book [namely, *An Introduction to Early Greek Philosophy*].

C. I wished to write directly from the texts of the early Greek philosophers themselves, and with the student, not the scholar, in mind.

—, as we learn by means of the Aptitude Method. (Page 107)

b. The argument—

P. I [John Mansley Robinson] wished to write directly from the texts of the early Greek philosophers themselves, and with the student, not the scholar, in mind.

C. I have consulted few specialist studies during the actual writing of the book [namely, *An Introduction to Early Greek Philosophy*].

—, as we learn by means of the Aptitude Method. (Page 152)

c. No argument, as best we can ascertain. (Page 164)

d. More than one of the above answers are correct. (Page 95)

e. Answers (a) through (d) are all incorrect. (Page 132)

EXERCISE SET 1

1.1 Question

In the sense in which it is used in this book, the word 'argument' means:

a. A reason given for something. (Page 157)

b. Something for which a reason is given. (Page 120)

c. A debate, in which reasons are given for and against opposing claims. (Page 97)

d. More than one of the above answers are correct. (Page 144)

e. Answers (a) through (d) are all incorrect. (Page 167)

1.3 *Answer (a)*

This answer is correct. But is it the only one that is? Return to page 161 for another look.

2.6 *Answer (e)*

At least one of the answers (a) through (d) is correct, so that (e) is incorrect. Return to page 116 to try again.

3.1 *Answer (b)*

Yes, one of the possibilities is that the arguments share the same premises but not the same conclusion. And so answer (b) is correct.

But is it the only answer that is correct? Return to page 130 to reconsider.

4.2 *Answer (e)*

At least one of the answers (a) through (d) is correct, so that (e) is incorrect. Return to page 101 to try again.

5.3 *Answer (d)*

No more than one of the answers (a) through (c) are correct, so that (d) is incorrect. Return to page 114 to try again.

6.6 *Answer (b)*

This answer is incorrect, because the illative 'shews [= shows] that' does not tell us that an argument is explanatory.

Return to page 119 to try again.

3.6 Answer (b)

This answer is incorrect, because the text does express an argument in which 'There is scarcely any part of the plant that is not put to some everyday use' is a premise. Return to page 108 to try again, this time using the Aptitude Method.

5.4 Question

Which of the following answers is best?

a. The following text expresses an argument that contains at least one false asserted premise:

> Since Alaska is further north than Kentucky, and Kentucky is further east than Colorado, Alaska is both further north and further east than Colorado.

(Page 147)

b. The following text expresses an argument that contains at least one false asserted premise:

> If Kansas is further north than Nebraska, and Nebraska is further north than Montana, then Kansas is further north than Montana.

(Page 106)

c. The following text expresses an argument that contains at least one false asserted premise:

> Were New York west of Chicago, and Chicago west of San Francisco, New York would be west of San Francisco.

(Page 119)

d. More than one of the above answers are correct. (Page 127)

e. Answers (a) through (d) are all incorrect. (Page 159)

1.10 Answer (b)

This answer is incorrect, as the word 'probably' is not an illative. It does not tell us that the person who uses it thinks that anything is a reason for anything else.

After writing a brief explanation why this answer is incorrect, return to page 68 to try again.

6.7 Question

Text:

> The circumstance of spiders of the same species, but of different sexes and ages, being found on several occasions at the distance of many leagues from the land, attached in vast numbers to the lines,[1] renders it probable that the habit of sailing through the air is as characteristic of this tribe,[2] as that of diving is of the Argyoneta. . . .

> —Charles Darwin, *The Voyage of the Beagle* (1860), ed. Leonard Engel (Garden City, New York: Doubleday & Company, Inc., 1962), Ch. VIII, p. 161.

This text expresses:

a. A verificatory argument, as we learn from the illative 'renders it probable that'. (Page 172)

b. An explanatory argument, as we learn from the illative 'renders it probable that'. (Page 164)

c. An argument that is both verificatory and explanatory. (Page 120)

d. More than one of the above answers are correct. (Page 132)

e. Answers (a) through (d) are all incorrect. (Page 96)

---

1. *I.e.,* the fine silken lines projected from a spider's spinners.
2. *I.e.,* spiders about three-tenths of an inch in length, and in their general appearance resembling a Citigrade.

5.8 Question

Text:

> As we shall see later, the nests of humming-birds, and the playing passages of bower-birds are tastefully ornamented with gaily-coloured objects; and this shews that they must receive some kind of pleasure from the sight of such things. . . .

> —Charles Darwin, *The Descent of Man and Selection in Relation to Sex* (1871); reprinted in *The Origin of Species by Means of Natural Selection and The Descent of Man and Selection in Relation to Sex* (New York: Random House, Inc., n. d.), Chapter III, p. 467.

Analysis:

P. The nests of hummingbirds and the playing passages of bowerbirds are tastefully ornamented with gaily colored objects.
C. They receive some kind of pleasure from the sight of such things.

Which of the following answers is best?

a. The argument is deductive, as the illative 'this shews that' and the word 'must' reveal. (Page 120)

b. The argument's premise does not make its conclusion certain. (Page 105)

c. The argument is invalid. (Page 165)

d. More than one of the above answers are correct. (Page 71)

e. Answers (a) through (d) are all incorrect. (Page 132)

6.8 Answer (b)

This answer is correct, because Holmes complies with Inspector MacDonald's explicit request ("why . . . ?") for an explanation of the proposition 'The police should abandon the case'.

But is this correct answer the best one? Return to page 110 to reconsider.

1.6 Answer (d)

No more than one of the answers (a) through (c) are correct, so that (d) is incorrect. Return to page 160 to try again.

2.5 Answer (d)

No more than one of the answers (a) through (c) are correct, so that (d) is incorrect. Return to page 97 to try again.

3.2 Answer (d)

No more than one of the answers (a) through (c) are correct, so that (d) is incorrect. Return to page 98 to try again.

4.9 Answer (e)

At least one of the answers (a) through (d) is correct, so that (e) is incorrect. Return to page 121 to try again.

5.11 Answer (e)

At least one of the answers (a) through (d) is correct, so that (e) is incorrect. Return to page 104 to try again.

6.5 Answer (c)

This answer is incorrect. Observe that Holmes asks Lestrade, "But *why* didn't the police see this mark yesterday?"

Return to page 126 to try again.

1.5 Question

Which of the following groups contains a word or expression that is *not* an illative?

a. Consequently   Since
    So   Therefore

(Page 98)

b. Certainly   As
    Thus   Hence

(Page 158)

c. Makes it probable that   For
    It follows from this that   Inasmuch as

(Page 147)

d. More than one of the above answers are correct. (Page 175)

e. Answers (a) through (d) are all incorrect. (Page 76)

2.2 Answer (a)

This is the correct answer. For the next question, proceed to page 118.

3.3 Answer (e)

This is the correct answer. To know that it is, you must have grasped that the relative pronoun 'which' in the text refers to 'the exact sciences', so that the text may be paraphrased thus:

What are called the humanities are more closely connected with poetry [than with the exact sciences—mathematics, physics, or chemistry] and are therefore less scientific than the exact sciences. The exact sciences are drier the more exact they are, for exact science is directed toward truth and only the truth.

The illatives 'therefore' and 'for' here work independently of each other, indicating different arguments, so that we can detect the two arguments expressed in the text—

A1.
P. What are called the humanities are more closely connected with poetry than with the exact sciences—mathematics, physics, or chemistry.
C. What are called the humanities are less scientific than the exact sciences.
A2.
P. Exact science is directed toward truth and only the truth.
C. The exact sciences are drier the more exact they are.

These arguments are not logically connected: they share neither premise nor conclusion, and neither's conclusion is the other's premise.

The next question is on page 109.

1.9 Question

Text:

> Certainly all human things are incapable of continuous activity. Therefore pleasure also is not continuous; for it accompanies activity. . . .

—Aristotle, *Nicomachean Ethics,* tr. W. D. Ross; in *The Basic Works of Aristotle,* ed. Richard McKeon (New York: Random House, Inc., 1941), X, 4, 1175ᵃ; p. 1099.

Which of the following answers is best?

a. The illative 'Certainly' tells us that this text expresses an argument whose conclusion is 'All human things are incapable of continuous activity'. (Page 163)

b. The illative 'Therefore' tells us that the text expresses the argument—

P. Certainly all human things are incapable of continuous activity.
C. Pleasure also is not continuous.

(Page 172)

c. The illatives 'Therefore' and 'for' work together to indicate the argument—

> P1. Certainly all human things are incapable of continuous activity.
> P2. It [pleasure] accompanies activity.
> C. Pleasure also is not continuous.

(Page 112)

d. More than one of the above answers are correct. (Page 127)

e. Answers (a) through (d) are all incorrect. (Page 153)

4.7 Question

Text:

> Coding is probably the most reliable of all our traditional documentation. The code at least represents what the program or procedure actually does. . . .

—Kenneth T. Orr, "Structured systems design: Blueprinting the Future", *Infosystems*, Vol. 24, No. 2 (February 1977), p. 73. (David Joyce)

Assuming that 'coding' and 'the code' refer to the same thing, this text expresses:

a. An inductive argument, as we properly discover by consulting the word 'probably'. (Page 159)

b. A deductive argument, as we must assume because the author uses no expressions that say whether he thinks his premise makes his conclusion probable or certain. (Page 113)

c. No argument. (Page 148)

d. More than one of the above answers are correct. (Page 74)

e. Answers (a) through (d) are all incorrect. (Page 170)

1.11 Question

Text:

> Museums have taken on many functions today. They are temples with the business problems of large corporations. They are arenas of education; they are also community centers and places of mass entertainment. . . .

—Robert Hughes, "Who Needs the Art Clones?", *Time,* Vol. 112, No. 35 (December 18, 1978), p. 94.

Which of the following answers is best?

a. The text expresses no argument. (Page 168)

b. The text expresses the following argument:

> P1. They [museums] are temples with the business problems of large corporations.
> P2. They [museums] are arenas of education.
> P3. They [museums] are also community centers and places of mass entertainment.
> C. Museums have taken on many functions today.

(Page 154)

c. The text expresses an argument, as we learn from the words 'have taken', in 'Museums *have taken* on many functions today'. For these words show that a proposition is being *asserted to be true,* which means that it is part of an argument. (Page 133)

d. More than one of the above answers are correct. (Page 100)

e. Answers (a) through (d) are all incorrect. (Page 71)

6.3 Answer (b)

This answer is incorrect, because it is possible for an argument to be both explanatory and inductive. An argument's being explanatory places no restrictions on whether it is deductive or inductive.

Return to page 138 to try again.

2.4 Question

Text:

> The origin of the Moors is involved [*i.e.,* enveloped, shrouded] in darkness: they were ignorant of the use of letters. . . .

—Edward Gibbon, *The Decline and Fall of the Roman Empire* (1776–1788), ed. Oliphant Smeaton (New York: The Modern Library, n.d.), Ch. XLI; Vol. 2, p. 550.

Hint: In the absence of evidence to the contrary, assume that the author thinks that his premises make his conclusion certain. Now, which of the following answers is best?

a. In this text, the colon is an illative that indicates the argument—

> P. They [the Moors] were ignorant of the use of letters.
> C. The origin of the Moors is involved [*i.e.,* enveloped, shrouded] in darkness.

(Page 109)

b. The argument that the text expresses is not defective and so does not require the addition of any unexpressed premise. (Page 143)

c. The proposition 'Their own written records are one way we have of knowing about the origins of a people' should be added to the argument as an unexpressed premise. (Page 77)

d. More than one of the above answers are correct. (Page 120)

e. Answers (a) through (d) are all incorrect. (Page 99)

5.9 Answer (b)

This is the correct answer. The argument is detectable only by the Aptitude Method and is inductive because of the expression 'more likely than not'. The argument is also valid, because its premise actually does make its conclusion probable.

Proceed to page 59 for the next question.

1.8 Answer (d)

No more than one of the answers (a) through (c) are correct, so that (d) is incorrect.
Return to page 78 to try again.

2.1 Answer (d)

No more than one of the answers (a) through (c) are correct, so that (d) is incorrect.
Return to page 160 to try again.

3.7 Answer (b)

Answer (b) is correct: the text expresses the argument analyzed. But is it the only correct answer?
Return to page 72 for another look.

4.6 Answer (d)

No more than one of the answers (a) through (c) are correct, so that (d) is incorrect.
Return to page 114 to try again.

5.10 Answer (d)

No more than one of the answers (a) through (c) are correct, so that (d) is incorrect.
Return to page 59 to try again.

6.1 Answer (e)

At least one of the answers (a) through (d) is correct, so that (e) is incorrect.
Return to page 149 to try again.

1.2 Answer (b)

This is the correct answer. To analyze an argument is to take it apart and to identify each part as a premise or conclusion.

Proceed to the next question, on page 161.

2.3 Answer (d)

This is the best answer, as answers (b) and (c) are both correct. Answer (a), however, is incorrect.

The next question is on page 91.

3.4 Answer (b)

This answer is incorrect, because the text expresses two arguments that share a premise.

Return to page 109 to try again. Analyze the arguments expressed in the text before trying to answer a question about their connectedness.

4.4 Answer (d)

No more than one of the answers (a) through (c) are correct, so that (d) is incorrect.
Return to page 123 to try again.

5.7 Answer (c)

This answer is incorrect, because the argument is not inductive.
Return to page 103 to try again.

6.6 Answer (d)

No more than one of the answers (a) through (c) are correct, so that (d) is incorrect.
Return to page 119 to try again.

1.7 Answer (b)

You're right in thinking that 'this fact that . . . leads to the conclusion that' is an illative but wrong in thinking that it indicates the argument analyzed in answer (b).

After writing on your answer sheet a brief explanation why this answer is wrong, return to page 70 and reexamine the text to see which proposition the illative identifies as a premise and which it identifies as a conclusion.

EXERCISE SET 4

4.1 Question

Which of the following answers is best?

a. The following text expresses a deductive argument:

> The fact that you drive an expensive car makes it highly probable that you're materialistic.

(Page 128)

b. The following text expresses an inductive argument:

> The fact that you drive an expensive car suggests that you're materialistic.

(Page 104)

c. The following text expresses a deductive argument:

> The fact that you drive an expensive car proves that you're materialistic.

(Page 146)

d. More than one of the above answers are correct. (Page 156)

e. Answers (a) through (d) are all incorrect. (Page 64)

1.12 Answer (d)

Presumably, you chose this answer because you think answers (a) and (b) are both correct. But only one is, and there is a part of the Aptitude Method that allows you to ascertain which. After you have ascertained that each proposition would plausibly be a reason for the other, and have searched the text without success for verbal clues to tell you which of the two is the conclusion the author had in mind, what is the next step?

Return to page 80 to try again.

3.6 Answer (a)

This is the correct answer, as the text expresses two arguments, and the conclusion of one is a premise of the other. Those arguments are—

A1.
>   P. There is scarcely any part of the [*Cocas nucifera*] plant that is not put to some everyday use.
>   C. *Cocas nucifera* is the most useful of all palms.

A2.
>   P1. *Cocas nucifera* provides wood for construction, fermented and unfermented drinks, oil for cooking, feed for cattle, and fertilizer.
>   P2. The dried coconut, or copra, finds its way into our American homes in the form of soap and margarine.
>   C. = A1-P.

The text being without illatives, we must use the Aptitude Method to find these arguments. '*Cocas nucifera* is the most useful of all palms' is a proposition for which it is plausible that 'There is scarcely any part of the plant that is not put to some everyday use', would be a reason, whereas it is not plausible that the former proposition would be a reason for the latter. This, then, gives us A1. And for 'There is scarcely any part of the plant that is not put to some everyday use' it is plausible that the propositions 'It provides wood for construction, fermented and unfermented drinks, oil for cooking, feed for cattle, and fertilizer' and 'The dried coconut, or copra, finds its way into our American homes in the form of soap and margarine' would be reasons. On the other hand, it is not plausible that the proposition 'There is scarcely any part of the plant that is not put to some everyday use' would be a reason for the latter two. This gives us A2. And so the text expresses the argument-chain analyzed above.

The next question is on page 72.

1.10 Answer (e)

This is the correct answer, since 'nevertheless', 'probably', and 'in all probability' are none of them illatives, as answers (a), (b), and (c) claim. Do not mistake words like 'nevertheless' (*e.g.,* 'however', 'notwithstanding', 'yet') for illatives. And, although expressions like 'probably' and 'in all probability' do tell us that their user regards some proposition as probable, they still are not illatives, since they do not tell us that he thinks that one proposition is a reason for another.

The next question is on page 90.

6.7 Answer (e)

This is the correct answer, since the others are all incorrect. The text expresses the argument—

P. Spiders of the same species, but of different sexes and ages, are found on several occasions at the distance of many leagues from the land, attached in vast numbers to the lines [*i.e.,* fine, silken lines projected from a spider's spinners].
C. The habit of sailing through the air is as characteristic of this tribe [namely, spiders about three-tenths of an inch in length, and in their general appearance resembling a Citigrade], as that of diving is of the Argyoneta.

—, as the illative 'renders it probable that' tells us. This illative also tells us that the argument is inductive.

But it does not tell us that the argument is verificatory, as it might just as well be used to indicate an explanatory argument. (Therefore, answer (a) is wrong.) Nor does it tell us that the argument is explanatory, as it might just as well be used to indicate a verificatory argument. (So, answer (b) is wrong, too.) And the argument probably is not both verificatory and explanatory, as answer (c) erroneously claims. Rather, the arguer is likely to think that his premise verifies, not that it explains, his conclusion; for the premise would plausbily verify, but not explain, the conclusion. The fact that different sexes and ages of spiders of the same species are found on several occasions many leagues from land, attached in vast numbers to silken lines, in no way would explain, or account for, the habit of sailing through the air being as characteristic of this species of spider as the habit of diving is characteristic of the Argyoneta. The premise would plausibly be evidence for, but not an explanation of, the fact. So, the premise has an aptitude to verify, but not to explain, the conclusion. From this (in the absence of more direct, verbal clues about what the arguer has in mind) we conclude that the argument is probably verificatory rather than explanatory.

Proceed to page 110 for the next question.

1.1 Answer (c)

This answer is incorrect, because, although answer (c) does give one of the senses of the word 'argument', it is not the sense in which that word is used in this book.

After writing on your answer sheet a brief explanation why this answer is wrong, return to page 81 to try again.

2.5 Question

Text:

Since a thought is a sentence and a sentence is a picture, a thought is a picture.

. . .

—Norman Malcolm, "Ludwig Josef Johann Wittgenstein", in *The Encyclopedia of Philosophy,* ed. Paul Edwards (New York: Macmillan Publishing Co., Inc. & The Free Press, 1967), Vol. 8, p. 331. (The author is expressing the views of Wittgenstein.)

Hint: In the absence of evidence to the contrary, assume that the author thinks that his premises make his conclusion certain. Now, which of the following answers is best?

a. The illative 'since' tells us that the text expresses the argument—

> P1. A thought is a sentence.
> P2. A thought is a picture.
> C. A sentence is a picture.

(Page 113)

b. The argument that this text expresses is obviously defective and needs an additional premise. (Page 66)

c. The proposition 'A picture portrays reality' should be added to the argument as an unexpressed premise. (Page 130)

d. More than one of the above answers are correct. (Page 86)

e. Answers (a) through (d) are all incorrect. (Page 149)

1.5 Answer (a)

The question asked you which of the groups contains something that is *not* an illative. An illative is an expression that indicates an argument. 'Consequently' is an illative, as are 'so', 'since', and 'therefore'. All of the words in this group, then, *are* illatives; and so answer (a) is wrong.

After writing a brief explanation why this answer is wrong, return to page 87 for another try.

3.2 Question

Which of the following answers is best?

a. The following text expresses two arguments that share a premise:

Abraham's check did not arrive in time, for one or the other of two reasons: (a) it was mailed late; or (b) the mail delivery was delayed.

(Page 112)

b. The following text expresses two arguments that share a conclusion:

The visitor was female, since her name was 'Mrs. June Grupp'. And, the same evidence shows that she is, or was, married.

(Page 136)

c. The following text expresses two arguments. The conclusion of one of them is also a premise of the other:

Abraham has plenty of work to do, because the shipment came in today. And Mrs. Grupp will see to it that he does the work on time, since the buyer demands that everything be ready promptly.

(Page 125)

d. More than one of the above answers are correct. (Page 86)

e. Answers (a) through (d) are all incorrect. (Page 148)

1.4 Answer (e)

At least one of the answers (a) through (d) is correct, so that (e) is incorrect. Return to page 121 to try again.

2.4 Answer (e)

At least one of the answers (a) through (d) is correct, so that (e) is incorrect. Return to page 91 to try again.

3.3 Answer (b)

This answer is incorrect. The text does not express two arguments that share a conclusion.
Return to page 115 to try again.

4.3 Answer (d)

No more than one of the answers (a) through (c) are correct, so that (d) is incorrect. Return to page 66 to try again.

5.6 Answer (e)

At least one of the answers (a) through (d) is correct, so that (e) is incorrect. Return to page 65 to try again.

6.4 Answer (e)

At least one of the answers (a) through (d) is correct, so that (e) is incorrect. Return to page 76 to try again.

1.11 *Answer (d)*

No more than one of the answers (a) through (c) are correct, so that (d) is incorrect.
Return to page 90 to try again.

2.2 *Answer (d)*

No more than one of the answers (a) through (c) are correct, so that (d) is incorrect.
Return to page 135 to try again.

3.8 *Answer (a)*

Sorry, this text does not express arguments that share a premise.
Return to page 134 to try again.

4.8 *Answer (e)*

At least one of the answers (a) through (d) is correct, so that (e) is incorrect.
Return to page 117 to try again.

5.2 *Answer (e)*

This answer is best, because all the others are incorrect. The correct answer would have been that an argument is sound if and only if (1) it is valid and (2) it contains no false, asserted premise.
Proceed to page 114 for the next question.

6.8 *Answer (e)*

At least one of the answers (a) through (d) is correct, so that (e) is incorrect.
Return to page 110 to try again.

4.2 Question

Which of the following answers is best?

a. The following text expresses an inductive argument:

> There can be no question that stratum A is younger than stratum B: it is nearer the surface.

(Page 127)

b. The following text expresses a deductive argument:

> The probability is over 9/10 that stratum A is younger than stratum B, since it's nearer the surface.

(Page 115)

c. The following text expresses an inductive argument:

> The probability that you're materialistic is about 0.872, given that you drive an expensive car.

(Page 152)

d. More than one of the above answers are correct. (Page 138)

e. Answers (a) through (d) are all incorrect. (Page 82)

6.2 Answer (a)

It is true that 'John can't keep food down', with the assistance of supplementary premises, could verify, but not explain, 'John is ill'; for it provides some evidence that John is ill but fails even partly to explain why. It is also true that 'John was exposed to a virus at a time when his resistance was low' could help either to verify or to explain 'John is ill'; for, if we did not already know that John is ill, this proposition could be a reason for thinking that he was; and, if we did already know that John is ill, this proposition would help to tell us why. Therefore, answer (a) is correct.

But is it the best answer? Return to page 137 to try again.

1.6 Answer (a)

This answer is incorrect. For the Aptitude Method does not tell us simply that whichever proposition expressed earliest in the text is the conclusion, and that the remainder are the premises. What it does tell us, that might be confused with this, is that, *if two propositions expressed in the text would plausibly be reasons for each other,* we should consider the one expressed earlier as the conclusion and the one expressed later as a premise. Do not neglect the italicized condition.

After writing on your answer sheet a brief explanation why this answer is wrong, return to page 160 for another try.

2.6 Answer (d)

This is the best answer, because answers (a), (b), and (c) are all correct.
The text contains the illative 'because' and expresses the argument—

P. The King [Philip IV of Spain] wanted to have Italian fresco painters at court.
C. Velázquez tried to tempt Pietro da Cortona to Madrid.

Now, this argument is defective in that it fails to provide any connection between *Italian fresco painters* and *Pietro da Cortona,* between *Philip's court* and *Madrid,* or between *King Philip IV of Spain* and *Velázquez.* But these defects are remediable by adding the unexpressed premises suggested in answers (a), (b), and (c). Answer (a) suggests adding 'Pietro da Cortona was an Italian fresco painter', and the suggestion is a good one, as the commentary to that answer shows (page 125). Answer (b) says that we should add 'Philip's court was in Madrid', which is correct, as the commentary to that answer makes clear (page 165). And answer (c) says that we should add 'Velázquez was an agent of King Philip IV of Spain'. The commentary to that answer details why it is correct (page 155). So, we add all three unexpressed premises to the argument, giving us—

P1. The King [Philip IV of Spain] wanted to have Italian fresco painters at court.
(P2. Pietro da Cortona was an Italian fresco painter.)
(P3. Philip's court was in Madrid.)
(P4. Velázquez was an agent of King Philip IV of Spain.)
C. Velázquez tried to tempt Pietro da Cortona to Madrid.

As this is the last question in Exercise Set 2, you are finished!

4.4 Answer (e)

The text expresses no argument at all, and so it expresses no deductive or inductive argument. Consequently, answers (a) through (d) are all incorrect.

You can ascertain that the text expresses no argument first by noting that it contains no illatives ('certainly' and 'probably' are not illatives) and second by attempting to use the Aptitude Method. It is not plausible that any of the propositions expressed in the text, even in league with others, would be a reason for another of them. Therefore, the Aptitude Method reveals no argument in the text. Since neither illatives nor the Aptitude Method permits us to discover any argument, we conclude that the text expresses none.

The next question is on page 105.

5.7 Question

Text:

> If a mirror-image of [object] *o* is indeed an imitation of *o*, then, if art is imitation, mirror-images are art. . . .
>
> —Arthur Danto, "The Artistic Enfranchisement of Real Objects: The Artworld", *Journal of Philosophy*, Vol. 61 (September 17, 1964), p. 571.

Analysis:

P1. A mirror-image of object *o* is indeed an imitation of *o*.
P2. Art is imitation.
C. Mirror-images are art.

Which of the following answers is best?

a. This is a valid deductive argument. (Page 76)

b. This is a valid inductive argument. (Page 169)

c. This is an invalid inductive argument. (Page 93)

d. More than one of the above answers are correct. (Page 64)

e. Answers (a) through (d) are all incorrect. (Page 150)

4.1 Answer (b)

The text expresses the argument—

        P. You drive an expensive car.
        C. You're materialistic.

The illative 'suggests that', which indicates the argument, also tells us that the arguer believes that the premise makes the conclusion probable. Hence, the argument is inductive, as answer (b) says.

But is this the only correct answer? Return to page 94 to reconsider.

5.11 Question

Text:

> Man comes to know God further by realizing that since there are powers less than oneself, it is logical that there would be a power greater than oneself. . . .
>
> —Student paper, Philosophical Problems, Augustana College, Sioux Falls, S.D., November 9, 1976, p. 3.

Analysis:

        P. There are powers less than oneself.
        C. There is a power greater than oneself.

Which of the following answers is best?

a. The premise makes the conclusion certain. (Page 163)

b. The premise is logically irrelevant to the conclusion. (Page 137)

c. The premise is both asserted and false. (Page 175)

d. More than one of the above answers are correct. (Page 149)

e. Answers (a) through (d) are all incorrect. (Page 86)

4.5 Question

Text:

>   The present author is a philosophical determinist. He would therefore, probably, although not certainly, choose the path of revolutionizing the law [instead of rejecting coercive persuasion as a criminal defense]. . . .

>   —Joshua Dressler, "Professor Delgado's 'Brainwashing' Defense: Courting a Determinist Legal System", *Minnesota Law Review,* Vol. 63, No. 2 (January 1979), p. 337, n. 15.

This text expresses:

a. A deductive argument, as we properly ascertain by consulting the illative 'therefore', together with the word 'certainly'. (Page 118)

b. An inductive argument, as we properly ascertain by consulting the illative 'therefore', together with the expression 'probably, although not certainly'. (Page 151)

c. A deductive argument, as we are compelled to assume; for the author employs no expressions that tell us whether he thinks his premise makes his conclusion probable or certain. (Page 167)

d. More than one of the above answers are correct. (Page 71)

e. Answers (a) through (d) are all incorrect. (Page 137)

5.8 Answer (b)

This answer is correct. The premise 'The nests of hummingbirds and the playing passages of bowerbirds are tastefully ornamented with gaily colored objects' does not make certain the conclusion 'They receive some kind of pleasure from the sight of such things'. For, even given that these birds place these objects in their nests and playing passages, it is possible that they do so by accident, or because they enjoy accumulating things whether gaily colored or not, or because they derive pleasure not from the sight but from the smell or feel of the objects, or because they think the colored objects will repel unwanted birds from their playing passages. So, (b) is a correct answer.

But is it the only such answer? Return to page 85 to find out.

1.3 Answer (b)

This answer is correct. But is it the only one that is? Return to page 161 for another look.

3.5 Answer (a)

This answer is incorrect: the text expresses no argument in which 'It is strange to make the supremely happy man a solitary' is a premise.

Return to page 122 to try again. This time attend more closely to the text's illatives.

4.9 Answer (d)

No more than one of the answers (a) through (c) are correct, so that (d) is incorrect. Return to page 121 to try again.

5.4 Answer (b)

This text expresses an argument—

P1. Kansas is north of Nebraska.
P2. Nebraska is north of Montana.
C. Kansas is north of Montana.

—whose premises are both false. But they are unasserted, as we can ascertain from the word 'if'. Therefore, this text expresses no argument that contains a false asserted premise. Answer (b), then, is wrong.

Return to page 83 to try again.

6.1 Answer (d)

No more than one of the answers (a) through (c) are correct, so that (d) is incorrect. Return to page 149 to try again.

1.12 Answer (a)

Although 'I [John Mansley Robinson] have consulted few specialist studies during the actual writing of this book [namely, *An Introduction to Early Greek Philosophy*]' would plausibly be a reason for 'I wished to write directly from the texts of the early Greek philosophers themselves, and with the student, not the scholar, in mind', the text does not express the argument analyzed in answer (a), as we learn from the Aptitude Method. Therefore, answer (a) is incorrect.

After writing on your answer sheet a brief explanation why this answer is wrong, return to page 80 to try again.

2.3 Answer (c)

This answer is correct. The text expresses the argument—

> P. The common people are human beings.
> C. The common people are sometimes inconstant.

(For details, see the commentary to answer (a).) But this is probably not all the author had in mind, since it is defective: it does not present the needed connection between the common people's *being human beings* and their *being sometimes inconstant*. One or more unexpressed premises are needed to provide this connection. Answer (c) says that 'All human beings are sometimes inconstant' is the unexpressed premise that should be added.

Is it? If this proposition is to be added to the argument as an unexpressed premise, it must satisfy the Method of Supply's following two requirements:

1. It is plausible that it, assisting the expressed premise, is a reason for the conclusion.
2. It is not likely that the author believes it to be false.

It is evident that the proposition satisfies the first requirement: 'All human beings are sometimes inconstant', together with the expressed premise 'The common people are human beings', is plausibly a reason for the conclusion, 'The common people are sometimes inconstant'. And it also satisfies Requirement (2), since it is not likely to be disbelieved by the author. Therefore, answer (a) is correct in saying that the proposition 'All human beings are sometimes inconstant' should be added to our analysis of the argument.

But is answer (c) the only one that is correct? Return to page 118 to try again.

3.6 Question

Text:

> *Cocas nucifera* is the most useful of all palms. There is scarcely any part of the plant that is not put to some everyday use. It provides wood for construction, fermented and unfermented drinks, oil for cooking, feed for cattle, and fertilizer. The dried coconut, or copra, finds its way into our American homes in the form of soap and margarine.

—Winifred Green Cheney, "You Thought There Were No New Ways to Cook a Chicken", *The National Observer* (October 12, 1974), p. 22. (Richard Chapman)

Which of the following answers is best?

a. The text expresses at least two arguments. One's conclusion is the other's premise. (Page 95)

b. The text expresses no argument in which 'There is scarcely any part of the plant that is not put to some everyday use' is a premise. (Page 83)

c. The text expresses no argument in which 'There is scarcely any part of the plant that is not put to some everyday use' is a conclusion. (Page 144)

d. More than one of the above answers are correct. (Page 127)

e. Answers (a) through (d) are all incorrect. (Page 159)

6.6 Answer (c)

This answer is incorrect, as the expression 'As we shall see later' modifies the argument's premise, 'The nests of hummingbirds, and the playing passages of bowerbirds are tastefully ornamented with gaily colored objects', not its conclusion, 'They [hummingbirds and bowerbirds] receive some kind of pleasure from the sight of such things'. But it could have told us whether the argument is verificatory or explanatory only if it had modified the conclusion. Consequently, the expression 'As we shall see later' cannot tell us whether the argument is verificatory or explanatory.

Return to page 119 to try again.

2.4 Answer (a)

This answer is correct, and it is the only one that is. The colon that appears in the text plays the part of an illative here, which means that the text expresses the argument—

P. The Moors were ignorant of the use of letters.

C. The origin of the Moors is involved [*i.e.*, enveloped, shrouded] in darkness.

Proceed to the next question, which you will find on page 97.

3.4 Question

Text:

DEMETRIUS . . .

> She is a woman, therefore may be wooed;
> She is a woman, therefore may be won;
> She is Lavinia, therefore must be loved.

—William Shakespeare, "The Tragedy of Titus Andronicus", ed. Sylvan Barnet (1964); in *The Complete Signet Classic Shakespeare,* ed. Sylvan Barnet (New York: Harcourt Brace Jovanovich, 1972), II, i, 82–84; p. 297.

Which of the following answers is best?

a. The text expresses no arguments that are logically unconnected. That is, all the arguments that the text expresses share a premise, or they share a conclusion, or one's conclusion is another's premise. (Page 167)

b. The text expresses no arguments that share a premise. (Page 93)

c. The text expresses no arguments that share a conclusion. (Page 129)

d. More than one of the above answers are correct. (Page 150)

e. Answers (a) through (d) are all incorrect. (Page 64)

2.2 Answer (c)

This answer is incorrect, because a premise does not differ from a presupposition in that a premise is a proposition that someone thinks is a reason for another proposition, whereas a presupposition is a proposition that is presupposed by another proposition *without anyone's thinking so.* One may think (correctly or incorrectly) that one proposition is presupposed by (*i.e.,* is a necessary condition of) another proposition. For example, someone who believes that Socrates is a father may (correctly) believe that this proposition presupposes the proposition 'Socrates is a parent'.

After writing on your answer sheet a brief explanation why this answer is wrong, return to page 135 to try again.

6.8 Question

Text:

> "Well, we're bound to take you on your own terms," said the inspector [Inspector MacDonald]; but when it comes to telling us to abandon the case—why in the name of goodness should we abandon the case?"
>
> "[Sherlock Holmes:] For the simple reason, my dear Mr. Mac, that you have not got the first idea what it is that you are investigating."

—Arthur Conan Doyle, *The Valley of Fear,* in *The Complete Sherlock Holmes* (Garden City, New York: Garden City Books,1930), p. 949.

The text expresses:

a. A verificatory argument, since Holmes expresses the premises in complying with Inspector MacDonald's request ("why in the name of goodness should we abandon the case?") for verification of the proposition 'The police should abandon the case'. (Page 145)

b. An explanatory argument, inasmuch as Holmes expresses the premises in complying with Inspector MacDonald's request ("why in the name of goodness should we abandon the case?") for explanation of the proposition 'The police should abandon the case'. (Page 85)

c. An argument that is both verificatory and explanatory. (Page 71)

d. More than one of the above answers are correct. (Page 155)

e. Answers (a) through (d) are all incorrect. (Page 100)

1.6 Answer (b)

This is the best answer, because, although it gives *only part* of what the Aptitude Method tells us, it is better than the other answers, which give nothing. The Aptitude Method does say that, if the text contains no proposition that would plausibly be a reason for any other proposition in the text, then the text expresses no argument. It also says that if one proposition expressed in the text would plausibly be a reason for a second, but not *vice-versa,* then the first is a premise, and the second the conclusion, of an argument; but if each of two propositions would plausibly be a reason for the other, then whichever is expressed earlier in the text is the conclusion and the other the premise.

Proceed to page 70 for the next question.

6.4 Answer (b)

This answer is incorrect, since someone's use of the illative 'because' would not tell us that his argument is explanatory. To see that 'because' can be used to indicate arguments that are verificatory, and not only explanatory, consider this text:

> "[Sherlock Holmes:] Both door and window were open for a very short time, however."
>> "[Inspector Martin:] How do you prove that?"
>> "Because the candle was not guttered."
>> "Capital!" cried the inspector. "Capital!"

—Arthur Conan Doyle, "The Adventure of the Dancing Men", in *The Complete Sherlock Holmes* (Garden City, New York: Garden City Books, 1930), p. 604.

'Because' indicates the argument—

P1. The candle was not guttered.
(P2. A candle is guttered only when exposed to a draft for more than a very short time.)
(P3. If both door and window were open, a draft would exist.)
(P4. Both door and window were open.)
C. Both door and window were only open for a very short time.

—, which is verificatory, not explanatory.

Return to page 76 to try again.

1.9 Answer (c)

This is the correct answer. The illative 'Therefore' tells us that 'Certainly all human things are incapable of continuous activity' is a premise, and that 'Pleasure also is not continuous' is the conclusion, in an argument. The illative 'For' tells us that 'It [pleasure] accompanies activity' is a premise, and that 'Pleasure also is not continuous' is the conclusion, in an argument. And since these two illatives here work together to indicate the same argument, rather than separately to indicate different arguments, they jointly indicate the argument analyzed in answer (c).

Note that the conclusion of this argument is identified as a conclusion twice—once by 'Therefore' and again by 'for'. Note too that, contrary to answer (a), 'Certainly' is not an illative.

Proceed to the next question, on page 68.

3.2 Answer (a)

The text—

> Abraham's check did not arrive in time, for one or the other of two reasons: (a) it was mailed late; or (b) the mail delivery was delayed.

—expresses the two arguments—

> A1.
>   P. It [Abraham's check] was mailed late.
>   C. Abraham's check did not arrive in time.
> A2.
>   P. The mail delivery was delayed.
>   C. = A1-C.

The illative 'for one or the other of two reasons:' tells us that the two premises belong to different arguments; for, although they *could* jointly be reasons for the conclusion, the author of this text offers them as alternative, not as coordinate or complementary, reasons for the conclusion. The text, then, expresses two arguments that share a conclusion, not a premise. This means that answer (a) is incorrect.

Return to page 98 to try again.

1.2 Answer (d)

No more than one of the answers (a) through (c) are correct, so that (d) is incorrect. Return to page 129 to try again.

2.5 Answer (a)

The text contains the illative 'Since' and expresses the argument—

P1. A thought is a sentence.
P2. A sentence is a picture.
C. A thought is a picture.

Answer (a) is incorrect, then, because its analysis of the argument interchanges the second premise and the conclusion.

After writing on your answer sheet a brief explanation why this answer is wrong, return to page 97 to try again.

3.7 Answer (c)

Answer (c) is correct: the text expresses the argument analyzed. But is it the only correct answer of the three?

Return to page 72 for another look.

4.7 Answer (b)

This answer is incorrect, because there is in the text an expression that helps to tell us whether the argument is deductive or inductive.

Return to page 89 to try again.

5.5 Answer (e)

At least one of the answers (a) through (d) is correct, so that (e) is incorrect. Return to page 75 to try again.

4.6 Question

Text:

> Certainly all human things are incapable of continuous activity. Therefore pleasure also is not continuous; for it accompanies activity. . . .
>
> —Aristotle, *Nicomachean Ethics,* tr. W. D. Ross; in *The Basic Works of Aristotle,* ed. Richard McKeon (New York: Random House, Inc., 1941), X, 4, 1175ᵃ; p. 1099.

This text expresses:

a. A deductive argument, as we properly ascertain by consulting not only the illatives 'Therefore' and 'for' but also the word 'Certainly'. (Page 171)

b. An inductive argument, as we properly ascertain by consulting the illatives 'Therefore' and 'for'. (Page 162)

c. A deductive argument, as we are compelled to assume; for the author employs no expressions that say whether he believes his premises make his conclusion probable or certain. (Page 135)

d. More than one of the above answers are correct. (Page 92)

e. Answers (a) through (d) are all incorrect. (Page 150)

5.3 Question

Which of the following answers is best?

a. If an argument is valid, then it is sound also. (Page 145)

b. If an argument is sound, then it is valid also. (Page 124)

c. An argument may be valid without being sound and sound without being valid. (Page 166)

d. More than one of the above answers are correct. (Page 82)

e. Answers (a) through (d) are all incorrect. (Page 156)

3.3 Question

Text:

> What are called the humanities are more closely connected with poetry [than with the exact sciences—mathematics, physics, or chemistry] and are therefore less scientific than the exact sciences which are drier the more exact they are, for exact science is directed toward truth and only the truth. . . .

—Gottlob Frege, "The Thought" (1918–1919), tr. A. M. and Marcelle Quinton, *Mind*, n. s. Vol. LXV, No. 259 (July 1956), p. 295.

Which of the following answers is best?

a. The illatives 'therefore' and 'for' here work together to indicate two premises and the conclusion of a single argument. (Page 131)

b. The text expresses two arguments that share a conclusion. (Page 99)

c. The text expresses two arguments. One's conclusion is the other's premise. (Page 120)

d. More than one of the above answers are correct. (Page 146)

e. Answers (a) through (d) are all incorrect. (Page 87)

4.2 Answer (b)

This text expresses the argument—

> P. It [stratum A] is nearer the surface [than stratum B].
> C. Stratum A is younger than stratum B.

The illative 'since' indicates the argument, and the expression 'The probability is over 9/10 that' informs us that the arguer thinks that the premise makes the conclusion very probable. But 'very probable' isn't the same as 'certain', and so the argument is not deductive but inductive. Answer (b), then, is wrong.

Return to page 101 to try again.

2.6 Question

Text:

> And it was certainly because the King [Philip IV of Spain] wanted to have Italian fresco painters at court that Velázquez tried to tempt Pietro da Cortona to Madrid. . . .

> —Joseph-Émile Muller, *Velázquez,* tr. Jane Brenton (London: Thames and Hudson, 1976), pp. 190–191.

Which of the following answers is best?

a. The text expresses an argument to which the unexpressed premise 'Pietro da Cortona was an Italian fresco painter' should be added. (Page 125)

b. The text expresses an argument to which the unexpressed premise 'Philip's court was in Madrid' should be added. (Page 165)

c. The text expresses an argument to which the unexpressed premise 'Velázquez was an agent of King Philip IV of Spain' should be added. (Page 155)

d. More than one of the above answers are correct. (Page 102)

e. Answers (a) through (d) are all incorrect. (Page 82)

5.9 Answer (e)

At least one of the answers (a) through (d) is correct, so that (e) is incorrect.
Return to page 74 to try again.

6.3 Answer (a)

This answer is incorrect, because it is possible for an argument to be both verificatory and inductive. An argument's being verificatory places no restrictions on whether it is deductive or inductive.
Return to page 138 to try again.

2.1 Answer (a)

This answer is incorrect, because it is not true that any unexpressed premise that we add to our analysis of an argument should plausibly be a reason, *by itself,* for the conclusion. Instead, it should plausibly *help any expressed premises* as reasons for the conclusion. The reason for this is that we add an unexpressed premise to an argument in order to fill in the gaps in the argument that the arguer had in mind—not to invent a different argument. Consequently, we seek not an unexpressed premise that would plausibly be a reason, by itself, for the conclusion, but one that would plausibly assist the expressed premises as reasons for the conclusion. (Of course, in the unlikely event that there are no expressed premises, any unexpressed premises we add to our analysis should plausibly be reasons, by themselves, for the conclusion.)

After writing on your answer sheet a brief explanation why this answer is wrong, return to page 160 to try again.

4.8 Question

Text:

> But—you can't explain anything by reasoning and consequently it is useless to reason.
>
> —Fyodor Dostoevsky, "Notes from the Underground", in *The Best Short Stories of Dostoevsky,* tr. David Magarshack (New York: Random House, Inc., n. d.), p. 234.

The text expresses:

a. A deductive argument, as we properly discover by consulting the word 'consequently'. (Page 155)

b. A deductive argument, as we properly discover by consulting the word 'can't'. (Page 165)

c. A deductive argument, as we must assume because the author uses no expressions that say whether he thinks his premise makes his conclusion probable or certain. (Page 141)

d. More than one of the above answers are correct. (Page 63)

e. Answers (a) through (d) are all incorrect. (Page 100)

2.3 Question

Text:

The common people are sometimes inconstant; for they are human beings. . . .

—Thomas B. Macaulay, *The History of England* (1848–1861), ed. Hugh Trevor-Roper (Harmondsworth, Middlesex: Penguin Books Ltd, 1968), V, p. 113.

Which of the following answers is best?

a. The illative 'for' tells us that the text expresses the argument—

> P. The common people are sometimes inconstant.
> C. They [the common people] are human beings.

(Page 142)

b. The argument that the text expresses is obviously defective, in that it needs an additional premise that is not expressed. (Page 162)

c. The unexpressed premise 'All human beings are sometimes inconstant' should be added to our analysis of the argument. (Page 107)

d. More than one of the above answers are correct. (Page 93)

e. Answers (a) through (d) are all incorrect. (Page 64)

4.5 Answer (a)

It is true that the text expresses an argument, that we ascertain whether it is deductive or inductive by consulting the author's expressions, and that we consult at least the illative 'therefore'. But it is not true that we consult the word 'certainly'. For it is part of the phrase 'probably, although *not* certainly' and so is used to help indicate that the writer has in mind probability *rather than* certainty. This is why we do not consult it and then conclude that the argument that the text expresses is deductive. Therefore, answer (a) is wrong.

Return to page 105 to try again.

5.4 Answer (c)

This text expresses the argument—

> P1. Were New York west of Chicago.
> P2. [Were] Chicago west of San Francisco.
> C. New York would be west of San Francisco.

—, whose premises are false but not asserted. Therefore, this text expresses no argument that contains a false asserted premise. So, answer (c) is incorrect.

Return to page 83 to try again.

6.6 Question

Text:

As we shall see later, the nests of humming-birds, and the playing passages of bower-birds are tastefully ornamented with gaily-coloured objects; and this shews that they must receive some kind of pleasure from the sight of such things.
. . .

—Charles Darwin, *The Descent of Man and Selection in Relation to Sex* (1871); reprinted in *The Origin of Species by Means of Natural Selection and The Descent of Man and Selection in Relation to Sex* (New York: Random House, Inc., n. d.), Chapter III, p. 467.

Which of the following answers is best?

a. This text expresses an explanatory argument, as we learn from the word 'must'. (Page 161)

b. This text expresses an explanatory argument, as we learn from the illative 'shews [= shows] that'. (Page 82)

c. This text expresses a verificatory argument, as we learn from the expression 'As we shall see later'. (Page 108)

d. More than one of the above answers are correct. (Page 93)

e. Answers (a) through (d) are all incorrect. (Page 171)

1.1 Answer (b)

This answer is incorrect, because something for which a reason is given is not an argument but a *conclusion*.

After writing on your answer sheet a brief explanation why this answer is wrong, return to page 81 to try again.

2.4 Answer (d)

No more than one of the answers (a) through (c) are correct, so that (d) is incorrect. Return to page 91 to try again.

3.3 Answer (c)

This answer is incorrect, since the text does not express two arguments one of whose conclusion is a premise of the other.

Return to page 115 to try again.

4.3 Answer (e)

At least one of the answers (a) through (d) is correct, so that (e) is incorrect. Return to page 66 to try again.

5.8 Answer (a)

This answer is correct. But is it the only one that is? Return to page 85 to try again.

6.7 Answer (c)

This answer is incorrect. The text expresses an argument that is either verificatory or explanatory, but not both.

Return to page 84 to try again.

1.4 Question

An *illative* is an expression that:

a. Indicates that the person who used the illative thought that one proposition is a reason for another. (Page 138)

b. Always comes after a premise but before a conclusion. (Page 148)

c. Always comes after a conclusion but before a premise. (Page 69)

d. More than one of the above answers are correct. (Page 165)

e. Answers (a) through (d) are all incorrect. (Page 99)

4.9 Question

Text:

But the operation of the wisest laws is imperfect and precarious. They seldom inspire virtue, they cannot always restrain vice. Their power is insufficient to prohibit all that they condemn, nor can they always punish the actions which they prohibit. . . .

—Edward Gibbon, *The Decline and Fall of the Roman Empire* (1776–1788), ed. Oliphant Smeaton (New York: The Modern Library, n. d.), Ch. XX; Vol. 1, p. 639.

This text expresses:

a. A deductive argument, as we properly discover by consulting the expressions 'cannot' and 'nor can'. (Page 166)

b. A deductive argument, as we must assume; for the author uses no expression that says whether he thinks his premises make his conclusion probable or certain. (Page 136)

c. No argument. (Page 153)

d. More than one of the above answers are correct. (Page 106)

e. Answers (a) through (d) are all incorrect. (Page 86)

3.5 Question

Text:

> Surely it is strange, too, to make the supremely happy man a solitary; for no one would choose the whole world on condition of being alone, since man is a political creature and one whose nature is to live with others. . . .

—Aristotle, *Nicomachean Ethics,* tr. W. D. Ross; in *The Basic Works of Aristotle,* ed. Richard McKeon (New York: Random House, Inc., 1941), IX, 9, 1169ᵇ; p. 1088.

The text expresses:

a. An argument in which 'It is strange to make the supremely happy man a solitary' is a premise. (Page 106)

b. An argument in which 'No one would choose the whole world on condition of being alone' is a premise. (Page 156)

c. An argument in which 'No one would choose the whole world on condition of being alone' is a conclusion. (Page 74)

d. More than one of the above answers are correct. (Page 142)

e. Answers (a) through (d) are all incorrect. (Page 132)

5.2 Question

An argument is sound if and only if:

a. It contains no false premise. (Page 67)

b. Its premises actually make its conclusion probable or certain, depending on which the arguer thinks they do. (Page 167)

c. It is valid and contains no false premise. (Page 133)

d. More than one of the above answers are correct. (Page 153)

e. Answers (a) through (d) are all incorrect. (Page 100)

4.4 Question

Text:

A being of higher faculties requires more to make him happy, is capable probably of more acute suffering, and certainly accessible to it at more points, than one of an inferior type. . . .

—John Stuart Mill, *Utilitarianism* (1861), ed. Oskar Piest (Indianapolis: The Bobbs-Merrill Company, Inc., 1957), Ch. 2, p. 13.

This text expresses:

a. A deductive argument, as we properly discover by consulting the expression 'certainly'. (Page 154)

b. An inductive argument, as we properly discover by consulting the expression 'probably'. (Page 164)

c. A deductive argument. For the text contains the conflicting expressions 'probably' and 'certainly', so that we cannot profitably consult the expressions that the author uses. (Page 144)

d. More than one of the above answers are correct. (Page 93)

e. Answers (a) through (d) are all incorrect. (Page 103)

6.1 Answer (b)

This answer is incorrect, because it would erroneously imply that the verificatory argument expressed in the text—

I knew that that plastic spoon melted, since it was placed within an inch of a flame, and plastic always melts when placed so near a flame.

—is explanatory; for the premises of that argument (namely, 'It [that plastic spoon] was placed within an inch of a flame' and 'Plastic always melts when placed so near a flame') explain its conclusion (namely, 'That plastic spoon melted').

Return to page 149 to try again.

1.7 Answer (c)

Ah, but there *is* an illative in the text, so we need not turn to the Aptitude Method to find the argument that the text expresses.

After writing on your answer sheet a brief explanation why this answer is wrong, return to page 70 to try again.

3.8 Answer (b)

This answer is correct. The text—

But, whether because of a growing general sentiment or because of Franklin's liberal influence, the [General] Assembly [of Pennsylvania] turned promptly to revision [of the test act]. . . .

—expresses the arguments—

A1.
    P. There was a growing general sentiment.
    C. The General Assembly of Pennsylvania turned promptly to revision of the test act.

A2.
    P. Franklin exerted a liberal influence.
    C. = A1-C.

—, as the illative 'whether because of . . . or because of' reveals. This illative tells us that alternate reasons are given for the same conclusion, so that the text expresses two arguments, with different premises but the same conclusion.

This is the final exercise in Set 3, so you're finished!

5.3 Answer (b)

This is the correct answer. An argument is sound if and only if (1) it is valid and (2) it contains no false asserted premise. Consequently, if an argument is sound, then it is valid also.

Proceed to the next question, on page 83.

2.6 Answer (a)

The expressed argument, indicated by the illative 'because' is—

P. The King [Philip IV of Spain] wanted to have Italian fresco painters at court.
C. Velázquez tried to tempt Pietro da Cortona to Madrid.

This is obviously defective. For one thing, it fails to provide any connection between *Italian fresco painters* and *Pietro da Cortona*. Perhaps an unexpressed premise would help. Answer (a) suggests 'Pietro da Cortona was an Italian fresco painter'. This satisfies both requirements of the Method of Supply, and so it should be added. Answer (a), then, is correct.

But is it the best answer? Return to page 116 for another look.

3.2 Answer (c)

The text—

> Abraham has plenty of work to do, because the shipment came in today. And Mrs. Grupp will see to it that he does the work on time, since the buyer demands that everything be ready promptly.

—expresses the two arguments—

A1.
    P. The shipment came in today.
    C. Abraham has plenty of work to do.
A2.
    P. The buyer demands that everything be ready promptly.
    C. Mrs. Grupp will see to it that he [Abraham] does the work on time.

The illative 'because' indicates A1, and 'since' indicates A2. As you can see, the conclusion of neither argument is a premise of the other. In fact, no proposition is common to them. Therefore, answer (c) is wrong when it says that the conclusion of one of the arguments is also a premise of the other.

Return to page 98 to try again.

5.6 Answer (c)

This is the correct answer. The text expresses a deductive argument, as we can ascertain by means of the word 'certainly', collaborating with two occurrences of the illative 'since'. Hence, for the argument to be valid, its premises must actually make its conclusion certain. And, as it happens, the premises, 'Everything in this bit of wax in the field of taste, smell, sight, touch, and hearing is changed' and 'The same wax nevertheless remains', do make certain the conclusion, 'That which, in this bit of wax, we recognize [as the same after the wax has been brought near the fire] cannot be anything I [René Descartes] observed by means of the (five) senses'. For given that everything that we can sense about the bit of wax has changed, although we can still apprehend that something about the wax remains the same, it is impossible that what we recognize is something we can sense (by means of the ordinary five senses). Consequently, the argument is valid. Therefore, it is a valid deductive argument, as answer (c) asserts.

Proceed to page 103 for the next question.

6.5 Question

Text:

> "[Sherlock Holmes:] But why didn't the police see this mark [namely, a bloody thumbprint on a whitewashed wall of a hall] yesterday?"
>
> "[Inspector Lestrade:] Well, we had no particular reason to make a careful examination of the hall. Besides, it's not in a very prominent place, as you see."

—Arthur Conan Doyle, "The Adventure of the Norwood Builder", in *The Complete Sherlock Holmes* (Garden City, New York: Garden City Books, 1930), p. 588.

This text expresses:

a. A verificatory argument. (Page 174)

b. An explanatory argument. (Page 154)

c. An argument that is both verificatory and explanatory. (Page 86)

d. More than one of the above answers are correct. (Page 166)

e. Answers (a) through (d) are all incorrect. (Page 144)

1.9 Answer (d)

No more than one of the answers (a) through (c) are correct, so that (d) is incorrect.
Return to page 88 to try again.

3.6 Answer (d)

No more than one of the answers (a) through (c) are correct, so that (d) is incorrect.
Return to page 108 to try again.

4.2 Answer (a)

This text expresses the argument—

> P. It [stratum A] is nearer the surface [than stratum B].
> C. Stratum A is younger than stratum B.

The illative ':' tells us which proposition is the premise and which the conclusion, whereas the expression 'There can be no question that' tells us that the arguer believes that his premise makes his conclusion certain. The argument, therefore, is deductive, not inductive, as answer (a) claims.
Return to page 101 to try again.

5.4 Answer (d)

No more than one of the answers (a) through (c) are correct, so that (d) is incorrect.
Return to page 83 to try again.

6.2 Answer (e)

At least one of the answers (a) through (d) is correct, so that (e) is incorrect.
Return to page 137 to try again.

1.3 Answer (e)

At least one of the answers (a) through (d) is correct, so that (e) is incorrect. Return to page 161 to try again.

3.7 Answer (a)

Answer (a) is indeed correct: the text expresses the argument analyzed. But is it the only correct answer?

Return to page 72 for another look.

4.1 Answer (a)

This text expresses the argument—

P. You drive an expensive car.
C. You're materialistic.

The illative 'makes it highly probable that', which indicates the argument, tells us that the arguer believes that the premise makes the conclusion highly probable. Consequently, the argument is not deductive, as answer (a) claims, but inductive.

Return to page 94 to try again.

5.5 Answer (d)

This is the best answer, as answers (b) and (c) are both correct.
Proceed to page 65 for the next question.

6.4 Answer (c)

This is the correct answer, because, like 'therefore' and 'because', neither 'since', 'so', nor 'for' tells us whether the argument it indicates is verificatory or explanatory.

Proceed to the next question, on page 126.

1.2 Question

To *analyze* an argument is:

a. To ascertain whether it is a good or a bad argument. (Page 159)

b. To divide it into all of its constituent propositions, saying which are the premises and which the conclusion. (Page 93)

c. To scrutinize it intently with the mind's eye, in order to apprehend the essential unity that makes its parts all parts of the same whole. (Page 143)

d. More than one of the above answers are correct. (Page 113)

e. Answers (a) through (d) are all incorrect. (Page 64)

3.4 Answer (c)

This is the correct answer, as the text expresses no arguments that share a conclusion. The illative 'therefore' occurs three times in the text, revealing these arguments:

> A1.
>> P. She [Lavinia] is a woman.
>> C. She may be wooed.
> A2.
>> P. = A1-P.
>> C. She may be won.
> A3.
>> P. She is Lavinia.
>> C. She must be loved.

A3 shares no proposition with A1 or A2 and so is not connected with either of them; hence, answer (a) is false. But A1 and A2 share the same premise, making answer (b) false also. This text, then, contains some connected and some unconnected arguments. But it expresses no arguments that share a conclusion, and so (c) is correct.

The next question is on page 122.

2.5 Answer (c)

The text contains the illative 'Since' and expresses the argument—

> P1. A thought is a sentence.
> P2. A sentence is a picture.
> C. A thought is a picture.

Answer (c) says that to this analysis should be added the proposition—

> A picture portrays reality.

Should this proposition be added to the argument? First of all, does the argument as it stands *need* another premise? No, it doesn't: the two it has are sufficient to make the conclusion certain, which (as the provided hint says) is probably what the author had in mind. The argument, then, is not defective as it stands and so does not need an additional premise. Consequently, answer (c) is wrong in saying that the above proposition should be added to the argument as an unexpressed premise.

After writing a brief explanation why this answer is incorrect, return to page 97 for another try.

EXERCISE SET 3

3.1 Question

When a text expresses more than one argument, it is possible that:

a. The text expresses only one of the arguments, the others remaining implicit. (Page 173)

b. The arguments share the same premises but not the same conclusion. (Page 82)

c. The arguments share the same conclusion but not the same premises. (Page 166)

d. More than one of the above answers are correct. (Page 143)

e. Answers (a) through (d) are all incorrect. (Page 158)

2.1 Answer (c)

This answer is not correct, because it is false that any unexpressed premise that we add to our analysis of an argument should plausibly assist any expressed premises to make the conclusion probable. For the arguer may believe that his premises make his conclusion not probable but certain. For instance, the arguer who says—

Socrates must be right-handed, since he's a stonemason.

—believes that his premises make his conclusion 'Socrates is right-handed' certain, not probable, as we learn from his use of the word 'must'. So, we would not be completing the argument as the arguer had it in mind if we were to add an unexpressed premise that, like 'Most stonemasons are right-handed', would plausibly help the expressed premise make the conclusion probable.

After writing on your answer sheet a brief explanation why this answer is wrong, return to page 160 to try again.

3.3 Answer (a)

This answer is incorrect. You are overlooking the fact that this part of the text—

. . . [what are called the humanities] are . . . less scientific than
the exact sciences which are drier the more exact they are . . .

—expresses not just one but two propositions. Perhaps this will become more apparent if we interpolate the phrase 'by the way' thus:

. . . [what are called the humanities] are . . . less scientific than the exact
sciences which [by the way] are drier the more exact they are. . . .

Once you see that this part of the text expresses not only the proposition 'What are called the humanities are less scientific than the exact sciences' but also 'The exact sciences are drier the more exact they are', it should be easy to see that 'therefore' and 'for' do not work together here to indicate the same argument but separately to indicate different arguments, and that the text expresses more than one argument.

Return to page 115 for another try.

1.12 Answer (e)

At least one of the answers (a) through (d) is correct, so that (e) is incorrect. Return to page 80 to try again.

3.5 Answer (e)

At least one of the answers (a) through (d) is correct, so that (e) is incorrect. Return to page 122 to try again.

4.3 Answer (b)

This answer is incorrect, because the illative 'because', while it does indicate the author's argument, does not tell us whether he thinks that the premise makes the conclusion certain or probable. 'Because' tells us that the author is offering the proposition 'Mankind is much more easily impressed by elemental forces in a primitive state of culture than later on, when intellectual consciousness and the faculty of reflection have attained a higher degree of maturity' as a reason for the proposition 'The action of music was far more direct in the case of ancient races than it is with us'. But it does not tell us whether that reason is supposed to make the conclusion certain or only probable. Some illatives (such as 'make it probable that' and 'proves that') do tell us that; but others (such as 'therefore' and 'since') do not.

Return to page 66 to try again.

5.8 Answer (e)

At least one of the answers (a) through (d) is correct, so that (e) is incorrect. Return to page 85 to try again.

6.7 Answer (d)

No more than one of the answers (a) through (c) are correct, so that (d) is incorrect. Return to page 84 to try again.

1.11 Answer (c)

The main thing wrong with this answer is that a proposition may be asserted to be true without being part of an argument: it is possible that an asserted proposition is neither a premise nor a conclusion. You will find examples of such assertions in the text of 1.10 Question, on page 68. So, we cannot infer that an argument is expressed merely from the fact that some proposition is asserted to be true.

The next thing wrong with this answer is that the occurrence of the words 'have taken' in a sentence or clause does not tell us that any proposition expressed by that sentence or clause is being asserted to be true. For example, those same words occur in the sentence 'Either museums have taken on many functions today or they will do so tomorrow', but that does not mean that the proposition 'Museums have taken on many functions today' is being asserted to be true. Nor would this be altered even if the words 'have taken' were emphasized.

In view of the foregoing, you may conclude that (c) is not correct.

After writing a brief explanation why this answer is incorrect, return to page 90 for another try.

5.2 Answer (c)

This answer is incorrect, because it would classify as unsound some arguments that ought to be classified as sound. For instance, if someone says—

> If my grandmother were a trolley, and if all trolleys had
> wheels, my grandmother certainly would have wheels.

—, his argument—

> P1. My grandmother were a trolley.
> P2. All trolleys had wheels.
> C. My grandmother would have wheels.

—is valid (since the premises actually make the conclusion certain, as the arguer intends) but has at least one false premise. According to answer (c), this argument would be classified as unsound. But it seems wrong to fault this argument because of its false premise, when that premise is not asserted to be true: in the text, both premises are entertained hypothetically, as the repeated word 'if' and the use of the subjunctive mood show. Consequently, this argument should be classified as sound rather than unsound; and that makes answer (c) wrong.

Return to page 122 to try again.

3.8 Question

Text:

> But, whether because of a growing general sentiment or because of Franklin's liberal influence, the [General] Assembly [of Pennsylvania] turned promptly to revision [of the test act]. . . .
>
> —Carl Van Doren, *Benjamin Franklin* (New York: The Viking Press, 1938), Ch. 25, p. 735.

This text expresses:

a. Two arguments that share a premise. (Page 100)

b. Two argument that share a conclusion. (Page 124)

c. Two arguments, of which one's conclusion is the other's premise. (Page 153)

d. More than one of the above answers are correct. (Page 76)

e. Answers (a) through (d) are all incorrect. (Page 163)

6.1 Answer (a)

This answer is not correct, since it would erroneously imply that the explanatory argument expressed in the text—

> The minor mode is essentially unstable, which is why pieces in the minor tend to have endings in the major. . . .
>
> —Charles Rosen, *The Classical Style* (New York: W. W. Norton & Company, Inc., 1971, 1972), p. 25.

—is verificatory; for the premise of that argument (namely, 'The minor mode is essentially unstable') does (with the help of an unexpressed premise like 'The endings of pieces are usually in a stable mode') verify its conclusion (namely, 'Pieces in the minor tend to have endings in the major').

Return to page 149 to try again.

2.2 Question

A premise differs from a presupposition in that:

a. A premise is a proposition that an arguer thinks makes (or helps to make) another proposition (namely, a conclusion) certain or probable. A presupposition, on the other hand, is a proposition that is not a reason, but a necessary condition, for another proposition. (Page 87)

b. A premise may be either expressed or unexpressed: if expressed it can be found either by means of illatives or the Aptitude Method; if unexpressed, it can be found by means of the Method of Supply. A presupposition, on the other hand, can only be unexpressed: it cannot be expressed. (Page 168)

c. A premise is a proposition that someone thinks is a reason for another proposition, whereas a presupposition is a proposition that is presupposed by another proposition without anyone's thinking so. (Page 110)

d. More than one of the above answers are correct. (Page 100)

e. Answers (a) through (d) are all incorrect. (Page 76)

4.6 Answer (c)

This is the correct answer. The text expresses the argument—

P1. Certainly all human things are incapable of continuous activity.
P2. Pleasure accompanies activity.
C. Pleasure also is not continuous.

To ascertain whether this argument is deductive or inductive, we first consult any expressions that indicate whether the arguer believed that his premises make his conclusion probable or certain. 'Certainly' is not such an expression, since it does not work together with 'therefore' and 'for' but instead helps to express P1. That leaves only 'therefore' and 'for'. These are illatives that do not reveal whether the author believes his premises make his conclusion probable or certain. So, we cannot consult any of the author's expressions to ascertain whether the argument is deductive or inductive. This means that, as answer (c) asserts, we must assume that the argument is deductive.

The next question is on page 89.

3.2 Answer (b)

The text—

> The visitor was female, since her name was 'Mrs. June Grupp'.
> And the same evidence shows that she is, or was, married.

—expresses the arguments—

A1.
    P. Her [the visitor's] name was 'Mrs. June Grupp'.
    C. The visitor was female.
A2.
    P. = A1-P.
    C. She [the visitor] is, or was, married.

The illatives 'since' and 'the same evidence shows that' indicate A1 and A2 respectively, while the latter illative tells us that A2's premise is the same as A1's. The two arguments, therefore, share a premise, not a conclusion as answer (b) asserts. That answer, then, is incorrect.

Return to page 98 to try again.

4.9 Answer (b)

This is the correct answer. The text expresses the argument—

P1. The wisest laws seldom inspire virtue.
P2. They cannot always restrain vice.
P3. Their power is insufficient to prohibit all that they condemn.
P4. Nor can they always punish the actions which they prohibit.
  C. The operation of the wisest laws is imperfect and precarious.

—, as we learn only by means of the Aptitude Method. We cannot rely on the arguer's expressions to find out whether this argument is deductive or inductive, as the only expressions in the text that might seem at first to have any bearing on the question are 'cannot' and 'nor can', which help to express premises P2 and P4. So, by default, we consider the argument deductive.

This is the final exercise in Set 4, so you are finished!

4.5 Answer (e)

At least one of the answers (a) through (d) is correct, so that (e) is incorrect. Return to page 105 to try again.

5.11 Answer (b)

This is the correct answer. Whether there are powers less than oneself has nothing to do with whether there is a power greater than oneself: one's being greater than some does not make it even probable that one is less than others. Suppose God were to recite this argument to Himself. Should it convince Him that there probably is a power greater than Himself? No, because the fact that there are powers less than God makes it neither certain nor even probable that there are any greater.

This is the last exercise in the set, so you are finished!

6.2 Question

Which of the following answers is best?

  a. The proposition 'John is ill' could be *verified but not explained* (in part) by the proposition 'John can't keep food down' but could be *either verified or explained* (in part) by the proposition 'John was exposed to a virus at a time when his resistance was low'. (Page 101)

  b. The proposition 'The sun will rise in the east tomorrow' could be *verified but not explained* (in part) by the proposition 'The earth rotates from west to east' but could be *either verified or explained* (in part) by the proposition 'The sun has risen in the east each morning for as long as anyone here can remember'. (Page 153)

  c. The proposition 'John ought to take this job' could be *verified but not explained* (in part) by the two propositions 'John's uncle advised him to take this job' and 'His uncle has never been wrong' but could be *either verified or explained* (in part) by the proposition 'This job would offer John all the advantages he wants without any disadvantages'. (Page 163)

  d. More than one of the above answers are correct. (Page 65)

  e. Answers (a) through (d) are all incorrect. (Page 127)

1.4 Answer (a)

This is the correct answer: an illative is a word or a longer expression that tells us the person who used it thinks that one proposition is a reason for another.

Proceed to the next question, on page 87.

3.7 Answer (e)

At least one of the answers (a) through (d) is correct, so that (e) is incorrect.
Return to page 72 to try again.

4.2 Answer (d)

No more than one of the answers (a) through (c) are correct, so that (d) is incorrect.
Return to page 101 to try again.

5.10 Answer (c)

This answer is incorrect, since the argument is not inductive.
Return to page 59 to try again.

6.3 Question

Which of the following answers is best?

a. No argument can be both verificatory and inductive. (Page 116)

b. No argument can be both explanatory and inductive. (Page 90)

c. No argument can be both verificatory and explanatory. (Page 157)

d. More than one of the above answers are correct. (Page 64)

e. Answers (a) through (d) are all incorrect. (Page 146)

1.10 Answer (a)

This answer is incorrect, since 'nevertheless' is not an illative. Like 'but', 'though', and 'however', it is an adversative conjunction, which does not tell us that anything is a premise or a conclusion in an argument.

After writing a brief explanation why this answer is incorrect, return to page 68 for another try.

5.8 Question

Text:

> As we shall see later, the nests of humming-birds, and the playing passages of bower-birds are tastefully ornamented with gaily-coloured objects; and this shews that they must receive some kind of pleasure from the sight of such things. . . .

—Charles Darwin, *The Descent of Man and Selection in Relation to Sex* (1871); reprinted in *The Origin of Species by Means of Natural Selection and The Descent of Man and Selection in Relation to Sex* (New York: Random House, Inc., n. d.), Chapter III, p. 467.

Analysis:

P. The nests of hummingbirds and the playing passages of bowerbirds are tastefully ornamented with gaily colored objects.
C. They receive some kind of pleasure from the sight of such things.

Which of the following answers is best?

a. The argument is deductive, as the illative 'this shews that' and the word 'must' reveal. (Page 120)

b. The argument's premise does not make its conclusion certain. (Page 105)

c. The argument is invalid. (Page 165)

d. More than one of the above answers are correct. (Page 71)

e. Answers (a) through (d) are all incorrect. (Page 132)

1.7 Answer (a)

This answer is mistaken, because 'Furthermore' is not an illative: it does not tell us that one proposition is supposed to be a reason for another. For example, in the fabricated text—

> "How are you feeling today, Maurice?"
> "My head aches, my stomach is upset, and my back is killing me. I have a cold coming on, moreover, and my throat is getting sore. Furthermore, my fingernails seem to be loose."

—, 'Furthermore' is used in the same sense as in the authentic text under examination, but it does not indicate an argument.

After writing on your answer sheet a brief explanation why this answer is wrong, return to page 70 to try again.

5.5 Answer (a)

This text expresses the argument—

P. Alabama is entirely east of Mississippi.
C. Alabama is also entirely east of Tennessee.

In the absence of any expressions telling us otherwise, we assume that this argument is deductive.

It is problematic whether the Method of Supply will permit us to add the proposition 'Mississippi is entirely east of Tennessee' as an unexpressed premise to the argument. Admittedly, this proposition is false: Mississippi is *not* entirely east of Tennessee. But is it so obviously false that the author would be likely to disbelieve it?

Fortunately, we can ascertain whether the argument is sound or unsound without having to solve this problem. For (1) either the proposition is so obviously false that the author of the text would be likely to disbelieve it, or it is not. (2) If it is, then the Method of Supply will not permit us to add it; and without it the argument is clearly invalid, since the expressed premise alone would be logically irrelevant to the conclusion. And if the argument is invalid, it is unsound. On the other hand, (3) if the proposition is not so obviously false that the author would be likely to disbelieve it, then the Method of Supply permits us to add it to the argument as an unexpressed premise. But it would then be a false, asserted premise, so that the argument would be unsound. Therefore, (4) in either case the argument turns out to be unsound. This means that answer (a) is incorrect.

Return to page 75 to try again.

4.8 Answer (c)

This is the correct answer. The text expresses the argument—

> P. You can't explain anything by reasoning.
> C. It is useless to reason.

To ascertain whether this argument is deductive or inductive, we must simply assume that the arguer believes that his premises make his conclusion certain. For there are only two expressions in the text that might seem at first to have any bearing on the question: 'can't' and 'consequently'. The former helps to express the premise and so in fact has no bearing on whether the arguer thinks that very premise makes the conclusion probable or certain. The latter is an illative that does not say whether the author believes his premise makes his conclusion probable or certain. Therefore, we cannot rely on any expressions that the arguer uses and are compelled to consider the argument deductive.

Proceed to page 121 for the next question.

6.4 Answer (a)

This answer is incorrect, because someone's use of the illative 'therefore' would *not* tell us that his argument is verificatory. To see that 'therefore' can be used to indicate explanatory, and not just verificatory, arguments, consider this text:

> In performing Soler's *Fandango,* I came to the conclusion that its length and the exaggerated repetition of certain passages robbed it of its maximum effect. Therefore I have abbreviated it. . . .

—Rafael Puyana, program notes for Mercury album SR90459.

The argument indicated by the illative 'therefore'—

> P. The length and exaggerated repetition of certain passages in Soler's *Fandango* robbed it of its maximum effect.
> C. I [Rafael Puyana] have abbreviated it.

—, is explanatory, not verificatory.

Return to page 76 to try again.

2.3 Answer (a)

The illative 'for' does appear in the text, and it does indicate an argument; but it does not indicate the argument analyzed in answer (a). The reason for this is that 'for' tells us that what precedes it is a conclusion and that what succeeds it is a premise. So, the text expresses the argument—

> P. They [the common people] are human beings.
> C. The common people are sometimes inconstant.

—, in which the premise and conclusion of the argument analyzed in answer (a) are transposed. Hence, answer (a) is incorrect.

After writing a brief explanation why this answer is wrong, return to page 118 to try again.

3.5 Answer (d)

This is the best answer, inasmuch as answers (b) and (c) are both correct. The illative 'for' indicates the argument—

> A1.
> > P. No one would choose the whole world on condition of being alone.
> > C. It is strange to make the supremely happy man a solitary.

—, in which 'No one would choose the whole world on condition of being alone' is a premise. Hence, (b) is correct. And the illative 'since' indicates the argument—

> A2.
> > P1. Man is a political creature.
> > P2. Man is a creature whose nature is to live with others.
> > C. = A1-P.

—, in which 'No one would choose the whole world on condition of being alone' is the conclusion. Hence, answer (c) is correct.

This text, then, expresses a two-argument chain. The word 'surely' tells us how probable the arguer thinks A1-P makes A1-C; that is why it does not appear in our analysis.

The next question is on page 108.

142

1.2 Answer (c)

To "apprehend the essential unity that makes [an argument's] parts all parts of the same whole" is to understand how the parts together make up, not just several distinct things, but one whole thing. But to do this is to understand how the argument may be put together, or synthesized; and synthesis is the *opposite* of analysis. Therefore, answer (c) is incorrect.

After writing an explanation on your answer sheet why this answer is wrong, return to page 129 for another try.

2.4 Answer (b)

The text expresses the argument—

P. The Moors were ignorant of the use of letters.
C. The origin of the Moors is involved [*i.e.,* enveloped, shrouded] in darkness.

(For further remarks on the analysis of this argument, see the commentary to answer (a).) And the hint provided with the question advises you, in the absence of evidence to the contrary, to assume that the author thinks that his premises make his conclusion certain. Therefore, if this argument were not to be defective, its one premise would have to make its conclusion certain—which it obviously does not do. For the premise talks about *being ignorant of the use of letters,* while the conclusion talks about *having origins that are enveloped in darkness,* and the argument provides no connection between these two concepts. So, the argument is defective and needs at least one unexpressed premise to make the needed connection. Answer (b) claims that the argument is not defective, and so it is incorrect.

After writing on your answer sheet a brief explanation why this answer is wrong, return to page 91 to try again.

3.1 Answer (d)

This is the best answer, because answers (b) and (c) are both correct. The remaining possibilities, not mentioned in answers to this question, are that: (1) the arguments share *both* premises *and* a conclusion; (2) the conclusion of one argument is a premise of another; and (3) the arguments are not logically connected with each other in any way—*i.e.,* they share no premise and no conclusion, and the conclusion of neither is a premise of the other.

Proceed to the next question, on page 98.

1.1 Answer (d)

No more than one of the answers (a) through (c) are correct, so that (d) is incorrect. Return to page 81 to try again.

3.6 Answer (c)

This answer is incorrect, because the text expresses an argument in which 'There is scarcely any part of the plant that is not put to some everyday use' is a conclusion.
Return to page 108 to try again, this time using the Aptitude Method.

4.4 Answer (c)

This answer is wrong for two reasons. First, 'certainly' and 'probably' do not here conflict, since they indicate what the author thinks about the probability of different propositions. 'Certainly' indicates the probability he attributes to 'A being of higher faculties is accessible to suffering at more points than one of an inferior type', whereas 'probably' indicates the probability he attributes to 'A being of higher faculties is capable of more acute suffering than one of an inferior type'.

And second, before we can ascertain whether the text expresses a deductive or an inductive argument, we must ascertain that it expresses an argument. Does it?
Return to page 123 to try again.

5.9 Answer (a)

The text contains the expression 'more likely than not', not 'more than likely'. Consequently, answer (a) is incorrect.
Return to page 74 to try again.

6.5 Answer (e)

At least one of the answers (a) through (d) is correct, so that (e) is incorrect.
Return to page 126 to try again.

1.8 Answer (b)

This is the correct answer. The two occurrences of the illative 'since' work together to indicate the same argument: the first occurrence indicates both the conclusion and the first premise, while the second indicates the conclusion and the second premise as well. The conclusion, 'It [the One] cannot be defined in terms of those things', is thus twice identified as a conclusion.

The next question is on page 88.

5.3 Answer (a)

This answer is incorrect, because an argument may be valid without also being sound. For instance, if someone says—

> Since my grandmother is a trolley, and since all trolleys
> have wheels, my grandmother must have wheels.

—, his argument—

P1. My grandmother is a trolley.
P2. All trolleys have wheels.
C. My grandmother has wheels.

—is deductive (because of the word 'must') and valid, since the conclusion actually is certain, relative to the premises. But the argument is not sound, as it contains the false asserted premise 'My grandmother is a trolley'. Answer (a), therefore, is incorrect.

Return to page 114 to try again.

6.8 Answer (a)

This answer is correct, because Holmes responds to Inspector MacDonald, who, since he does not believe that the police ought to abandon the case, implicitly requests verification when he asks, "Why in the name of goodness should we abandon the case?" This is like a parent responding to a resisting child who, when told to wear his mittens, implicitly requests verification by asking, "Why should I?"

But is this admittedly correct answer the best one? Return to page 110 to reconsider.

1.10 Answer (d)

No more than one of the answers (a) through (c) are correct, so that (d) is incorrect. Return to page 68 to try again.

3.3 Answer (d)

No more than one of the answers (a) through (c) are correct, so that (d) is incorrect. Return to page 115 to try again.

4.1 Answer (c)

The text expresses the argument—

        P. You drive an expensive car.
        C. You're materialistic.

The illative 'proves', which indicates the argument, also tells us that the arguer thinks that the premise makes the conclusion certain. So, the argument is deductive, as answer (c) says.

But is this the only correct answer? Return to page 94 to reconsider.

5.6 Answer (d)

No more than one of the answers (a) through (c) are correct, so that (d) is incorrect. Return to page 65 to try again.

6.3 Answer (e)

This is the correct answer, inasmuch as all the others are incorrect. The next question is on page 76.

1.5 Answer (c)

The question asked you which of the groups contains something that is *not* an illative. An illative is an expression that indicates an argument. 'Makes it probable that', 'it follows that', 'for', and 'inasmuch as' are all illatives. All of the words in this group, then, *are* illatives; and so (a) is wrong.

After writing a brief explanation why this answer is wrong, return to page 87 for another try.

4.3 Answer (a)

This is the correct answer, since, in order properly to discover that this argument is deductive, we must consult the fact that the expression 'It is beyond all question that' tells us that the arguer believes that the proposition 'The action of music was far more direct in the case of ancient races than it is with us' is certain.

That is not *all* we must consult, though. For 'It is beyond all question that' is not an illative: it does not tell us that one thing is supposed to be a reason for another. And so it does not tell us that the text expresses an argument. To learn that, we must consult the illative 'because'. Each of these two expressions contributes something to our knowledge that the other does not: 'because' tells us that the author is arguing and identifies the premise and conclusion but does not tell us whether he thinks the premise makes the conclusion probable or certain; 'It is beyond all question that', on the other hand, does not tell us that the author is arguing, or what his premise or conclusion is, but it does tell us that he thinks (the conclusion) 'The action of music was far more direct in the case of ancient races than it is with us' is certain. It is these two expressions together that permit us to learn that the argument is deductive.

The next question is on page 123.

5.4 Answer (a)

This text expresses an argument—

      P1. Alaska is further north than Kentucky.
      P2. Kentucky is further east than Colorado.
      C. Alaska is both further north and further east than Colorado.

—whose premises are all asserted and true. Hence, answer (a) is incorrect.
Return to page 83 to try again.

1.4 Answer (b)

This answer is incorrect, because it is *only sometimes* true that an illative comes after a premise but before a conclusion. Illatives like 'therefore', 'so', and 'hence' do ordinarily follow a premise and precede a conclusion. For instance, in the text—

All men are mortal, and Socrates is a man. So, Socrates is mortal.

—, the illative 'so' follows the premise 'Socrates is a man' and precedes the conclusion 'Socrates is mortal'. But illatives like 'for', 'since', and 'because' ordinarily precede a premise. For instance, in the text—

Socrates is mortal; for he is a man, and all men are mortal.

—, the illative 'for' follows a conclusion rather than a premise and precedes a premise rather than a conclusion. So, it is not true that an illative always comes after a premise but before a conclusion.

After writing on your answer sheet a brief explanation why this answer is wrong, return to page 121 to try again.

3.2 Answer (e)

This is the correct answer, as all the others are wrong. The next question is on page 115.

4.7 Answer (c)

This answer is incorrect, because the text does express an argument, although it does not indicate that argument by means of any illative.
Return to page 89 to try again.

5.1 Answer (d)

No more than one of the answers (a) through (c) are correct, so that (d) is incorrect.
Return to page 168 to try again.

1.6 *Answer (e)*

At least one of the answers (a) through (d) is correct, so that (e) is incorrect. Return to page 160 to try again.

2.5 *Answer (e)*

This is the correct answer, because all the others are wrong. Answer (a) is wrong because it offers a mistaken analysis of the argument expressed by the text; answers (b) and (c) are wrong because they either say or presuppose that the argument that the text expresses is defective as it stands and so needs one or more additional premises.

The next question is on page 116.

5.11 *Answer (d)*

No more than one of the answers (a) through (c) are correct, so that (d) is incorrect. Return to page 104 to try again.

EXERCISE SET 6

6.1 Question

Which of the following answers is best?

a. A verificatory argument is one whose premises verify its conclusion. (Page 134)

b. An explanatory argument is one whose premises explain its conclusion. (Page 123)

c. An explanatory argument is one whose premises the arguer thinks explain its conclusion. (Page 168)

d. More than one of the above answers are correct. (Page 106)

e. Answers (a) through (d) are all incorrect. (Page 92)

2.1 Answer (e)

This is the correct answer, as all the others are wrong. Any unexpressed premise that we add to our analysis of an argument should plausibly be a reason, not by itself, but assisting any expressed premises as reasons for the conclusion (*i.e.,* helping to make the conclusion probable or certain, depending on what the arguer has in mind).

Proceed to page 135 for the next question.

3.4 Answer (d)

No more than one of the answers (a) through (c) are correct, so that (d) is incorrect. Return to page 109 to try again.

4.6 Answer (e)

At least one of the answers (a) through (d) is correct, so that (e) is incorrect. Return to page 114 to try again.

5.7 Answer (e)

This is the correct answer, since all the others are wrong. The argument is deductive, as we must assume ('if' and 'then' being illatives that do not tell us whether the arguer thinks his premises make his conclusion probable or certain). This suffices to exclude answers (b) and (c). Answer (a) is excluded by the fact that the argument is invalid, because the premises do not make the conclusion certain. For even on the suppositions that a mirror-image of object *o* is an imitation of *o,* and that art is imitation (*i.e.,* that every work of art is an imitation of some object), it remains possible that mirror-images are *not* art. For although art is imitation, imitation may not be art (*i.e.,* although every work of art is an imitation of some object, maybe not every imitation of some object is a work of art); so that mirror-images may not be works of art. In fact, given the premises, it is no more probable than improbable that mirror-images are art. For given that a mirror-image of object *o* is an imitation of *o,* and given that every work of art is an imitation of some object, it is no more likely that every mirror-image is a work of art than it is that some—or even all—are not. The argument, then, is invalid, so that answer (a), too, is incorrect.

Proceed to the next question, on page 85.

1.3 Answer (c)

This answer is correct. But is it the only one that is?
Return to page 161 for another look.

4.5 Answer (b)

This is the correct answer. The text contains the illative 'therefore', followed immediately by the expression 'probably, although not certainly'. Hence, it expresses the argument—

P. The present author [Joshua Dressler] is a philosophical determinist.
C. He would choose the path of revolutionizing the law instead of rejecting coercive persuasion as a criminal defense.

Whereas 'therefore' both informs us that the writer is arguing and identifies his premise and conclusion, 'probably, although not certainly' tells us that he thinks his conclusion is probable but not certain. Working together, these expressions tell us that the author thinks his premise makes his conclusion probable. This suffices to tell us that the argument is inductive.

The next question is on page 114.

5.5 Answer (b)

This text expresses the argument—

P. Hawaii were Wyoming.
C. Hawaii would have no coastline.

—, to which the unexpressed premise 'Wyoming has no coastline' must be added. The argument that the author has in mind is deductive (we assume, in the absence of expressions that tell us otherwise) and valid, since the premises—expressed and unexpressed—jointly make the conclusion certain. The explicit premise is entertained hypothetically, but not asserted, as we learn from the word 'if'; but the unexpressed premise is asserted, precisely because it is unexpressed. The expressed premise is obviously false, but the unexpressed one is true. The argument, then, is free of false asserted premises. Hence, the argument is sound, since it is valid and has no false asserted premise. Answer (b), then, is correct.

But is it the only correct answer? Return to page 75 to reconsider.

1.12 Answer (b)

The text contains no illative, so we must depend on the Aptitude Method to learn whether it expresses an argument. As it happens, not only would 'I [John Mansley Robinson] have consulted few specialist studies during the actual writing of the book [namely, *An Introduction to Early Greek Philosophy*]' plausibly be a reason for 'I wished to write directly from the texts of the early Greek philosophers themselves, and with the student, not the scholar, in mind', but the second of these propositions would also plausibly be a reason for the first. There are no other clues in the text to suggest which proposition the author has in mind as his conclusion, so we assume that the proposition expressed earlier—namely, 'I [John Mansley Robinson] have consulted few specialist studies during the actual writing of this book [namely, *An Introduction to Early Greek Philosophy*]'—is his conclusion. This means that the text expresses the argument analyzed in answer (b), so that (b) is the correct answer.

This is the final question in Exercise Set 1, so you're finished!

4.2 Answer (c)

This text expresses the argument—

> P. You drive an expensive car.
> C. You're materialistic.

The illative 'given that' indicates the argument, whereas the expression 'The probability that . . . is about 0.872' tells us that the arguer believes that the premise confers on the conclusion a probability of about 0.872. The argument, then, is inductive, as answer (c) says. Hence, answer (c) is correct.

Proceed to page 66 for the next question.

5.10 Answer (a)

The argument is deductive, but not for the reason given in answer (a). The text does not employ the word 'definitely'; and the presence of the word 'not', even when given an emphasis missing from the text, has no bearing on whether the argument is deductive or inductive. Consequently, the argument is not deductive for the reason given in answer (a). Instead, we must assume it is deductive, because there are no expressions in the text to tell us otherwise.

Return to page 59 to try again.

1.9 Answer (e)

At least one of the answers (a) through (d) is correct, so that (e) is incorrect.
Return to page 88 to try again.

3.8 Answer (c)

No, the text does not express any arguments, of which one's conclusion is the other's premise.
Return to page 134 to try again.

4.9 Answer (c)

This answer is incorrect. For the text does express an argument, although no illative indicates it.
Return to page 121 to try again.

5.2 Answer (d)

No more than one of the answers (a) through (c) are correct, so that (d) is incorrect.
Return to page 122 to try again.

6.2 Answer (b)

It is false that 'The earth rotates from west to east' could help to verify *but not explain* 'The sun will rise in the east tomorrow'; for, with the assistance of a few supplementary premises, it could also explain it: the fact that the earth rotates from west to east is part of the reason why the sun will rise in the east tomorrow. It is also false that 'The sun has risen in the east each morning for as long as anyone here can remember' could help either to verify *or explain* 'The sun will rise in the east tomorrow'; for it could not help to explain it: it does not give even part of the reason why the sun will rise in the east tomorrow. Consequently, answer (b) is incorrect.
Return to page 137 to try again.

1.11 Answer (b)

Very good! This is the correct answer. The text does express the argument analyzed in this answer, as we discover not through any illatives but through the Aptitude Method. It is plausible that 'Museums are temples with the business problems of large corporations', in conjunction with 'Museums are arenas of education' and 'Museums are also community centers and places of mass entertainment', is a reason for 'Museums have taken on many functions today'. And no other combination of possible premises and conclusions would also be plausible. Therefore, the Aptitude Method uncovers for us the argument analyzed in answer (b).

Proceed to the next question, on page 80.

4.4 Answer (a)

'Certainly' does tell us that the author thinks that 'A being of higher faculties is accessible to suffering at more points than one of an inferior type' is certain. But it tells us neither that that proposition is a reason for anything, nor that anything is a reason for it. Does any other expression in the text tell us this? Can we learn it by means of the Aptitude Method? Only if the answer to one of these two questions is affirmative can we learn that the text expresses a deductive argument.

Return to page 123 to try again.

6.5 Answer (b)

This is the correct answer. When Holmes asks Lestrade, "But why didn't the police see this mark [namely, a bloody thumbprint on a whitewashed wall of a hall] yesterday?", he requests an explanation, not a verification, of the police's failure to notice the mark. When he responds to Holmes, Lestrade complies with his request: he offers the explanation Holmes asked for. Hence, he thinks that his premises—

P1. We [the police] had no particular reason to make a careful examination of the hall.
P2. It [namely, the bloody thumbprint] is not in a very prominent place, as you see.

—explain his conclusion, 'The police didn't see this mark [namely, a bloody thumbprint on a whitewashed wall] yesterday'. His argument, then, is explanatory, not verificatory.

Proceed to the next question, on page 119.

2.6 Answer (c)

The expressed argument, indicated by the illative 'because' is—

P. The King [Philip IV of Spain] wanted to have Italian fresco painters at court.
C. Velázquez tried to tempt Pietro da Cortona to Madrid.

This is obviously defective. For one thing, it fails to provide any connection between *King Philip IV of Spain* and *Velázquez*. Perhaps an unexpressed premise would help. Answer (c) suggests 'Velázquez was an agent of King Philip IV of Spain'. This satisfies both requirements of the Method of Supply, and so it should be added. Answer (c), then, is correct.

But is it the best answer? Return to page 116 for another look.

4.8 Answer (a)

'Consequently' is an illative that, like 'therefore' and 'since', tells us only that one proposition is offered as a reason for another. It does not also tell us whether the arguer thinks his premise makes his conclusion probable or certain. So, we cannot consult 'consequently' to find out whether the argument expressed in the text is deductive or inductive. For this reason, answer (a) is wrong.

Return to page 117 to try again.

6.8 Answer (d)

This is the best answer, as answers (a), (b), and (c) are correct. Inspector MacDonald does not believe that the police should abandon the case. Consequently, he asks Holmes for verification of the proposition that they should. So, answer (a) is correct. But, instead of explicitly requesting verification (*e.g.,* "How do you prove that we should?"), he requests verification implicitly while explicitly asking for an explanation ("Why in the name of goodness should we abandon the case?"). This means that answer (b) is correct, too. Hence, Inspector MacDonald requests, partly implicitly and partly explicitly, premises that will not only verify but also explain the conclusion. Such a double request is common when the conclusion either is, or could correctly be, expressed by means of an 'ought'- or 'should'-clause. Since Holmes complies with both the request for verification and the request for explanation, he expresses both a verificatory and an explanatory argument. This means that answer (c) is correct, too.

This is the last question in Exercise Set 6, so you are finished!

1.8 Answer (e)

At least one of the answers (a) through (d) is correct, so that (e) is incorrect.
Return to page 78 to try again.

2.2 Answer (a)

This is the correct answer. For the next question, proceed to page 118.

3.5 Answer (b)

It is true that the text expresses an argument in which 'No one would choose the whole world on condition of being alone' is a premise: the illative 'for' tells us that. Answer (b), then, is correct. But is it the only correct answer?
Return to page 122 to try again.

4.1 Answer (d)

This is the best answer, because answers (b) and (c) are both correct.
Proceed to the next question, on page 101.

5.3 Answer (e)

At least one of the answers (a) through (d) is correct, so that (e) is incorrect.
Return to page 114 to try again.

6.4 Answer (d)

No more than one of the answers (a) through (c) are correct, so that (d) is incorrect.
Return to page 76 to try again.

1.1 Answer (a)

This answer is incorrect, because a reason given for something is a *premise;* and, although 'premise' is one of the meanings the word 'argument' may have, that is not the sense in which 'argument' is used in this book.

After writing on your answer sheet a brief explanation why this answer is wrong, return to page 81 to try again.

5.6 Answer (a)

You are right in thinking that the argument is deductive. The word 'certainly' helps to tell us that. But is the argument really invalid? Do the premises fail to make the conclusion certain? Given that everything that we can sense about the bit of wax has changed, although we can still apprehend that something about the wax is the same, is it possible that what we recognize is something we can sense? Remember, your job at present is not to say whether you *believe* the conclusion, but whether the premises would make the conclusion certain.

Return to page 65 to try again.

6.3 Answer (c)

This answer is incorrect, because it is possible for the same argument to be both verificatory and explanatory. For it is possible for the author to have in mind the same premises' both verifying and explaining a conclusion. For instance, in this exchange—

A: In some Indian nations adjoining Hudson's Bay, children were obligated to strangle their aged parents.

B: That's hard to believe. Why would they do a thing like that?

A: Because when the parents became too old to support themselves, they did not wish to continue living, and so they commanded their children to strangle them.

—, B does not believe what A has said and so requests a verification that would also be an explanation. B's attitude seems to be that only if the proposition can be adequately explained will he believe it. A offers premises to meet this double challenge: they are intended not only to explain but also to verify the Indians' being obligated to strangle their parents. So, the same argument is both verificatory and explanatory. Answer (c), therefore, is incorrect.

Return to page 138 to try again.

1.5 Answer (b)

Although 'thus', 'as', and 'hence' are illatives, 'certainly' is not. It tells us that someone thinks that something is certain, but not whether he thinks it is the premise or the conclusion of an argument.

This group does contain a word that is not an illative, and it is the only one that does. So the correct answer to the question is (b), which you selected. Keep up the good work—on page 160, where you will find the next question.

2.2 Answer (a)

This is the correct answer. For the next question, proceed to page 118.

3.1 Answer (e)

At least one of the answers (a) through (d) is correct, so that (e) is incorrect. Return to page 130 to try again.

5.1 Answer (b)

This answer is incorrect, because an *in*valid argument's premises may make its conclusion certain. For example, if someone says—

> Three is greater than two, and two is greater than one. In view of this, it is likely that three is greater than one.

—, the premises of his argument—

> P1. Three is greater than two.
> P2. Two is greater than one.
> C. Three is greater than one.

—actually make its conclusion certain; and yet the argument is invalid.
Return to page 168 to try again.

1.2 Answer (a)

To ascertain whether an argument is good or bad is to *evaluate* it. But evaluation and analysis are not the same. An argument may, of course, be evaluated as well as analyzed; but the two activities—analysis and evaluation—are different.

After explaining on your answer sheet why this answer is wrong, return to page 129 for another try.

3.6 Answer (e)

At least one of the answers (a) through (d) is correct, so that (e) is incorrect. Return to page 108 to try again.

4.7 Answer (a)

This is the correct answer. The text expresses an argument, as is discoverable only by means of the Aptitude Method: 'probably', although it tells us that the author thinks that something is probable, is not an illative. The argument is—

P. The code at least represents what the program or procedure actually does.
C. Coding is the most reliable of all our traditional documentation.

—, to which unexpressed premises (*e.g.,* 'Representing what the program or procedure actually does is a criterion of reliability for traditional documentation') must be added. 'Probably' informs us that the author thinks that the proposition 'Coding is the most reliable of all our traditional documentation' (which is the conclusion) is probable but not certain. Therefore, the argument is inductive.

The next question is on page 117.

5.4 Answer (e)

This is the correct answer, as none of the texts in answers (a) through (c) expresses an argument with a false asserted premise.

The next question is on page 75.

1.6 Question

To ascertain whether a text containing no illatives expresses an argument, we employ the Aptitude Method, which tells us that:

a. Whichever proposition is expressed earliest in the text is the conclusion, and the remainder are the premises. (Page 102)

b. If the text contains no proposition that would plausibly be a reason for any other proposition in the text, then the text expresses no argument. (Page 111)

c. Whichever proposition is not likely to be disbelieved by the author is a premise in an argument expressed by the text. (Page 170).

d. More than one of the above answers are correct. (Page 86)

e. Answers (a) through (d) are all incorrect. (Page 149)

EXERCISE SET 2

2.1 Question

Any unexpressed premise that we add to our analysis of an argument should plausibly:

a. Be a reason, by itself, for the conclusion. (Page 117)

b. Assist any expressed premises to make the conclusion certain. (Page 72)

c. Assist any expressed premises to make the conclusion probable. (Page 131)

d. More than one of the above answers are correct. (Page 92)

e. Answers (a) through (d) are all incorrect. (Page 150)

5.9 *Answer (d)*

No more than one of the answers (a) through (c) are correct, so that (d) is incorrect. Return to page 74 to try again.

1.3 Question

Which of the following answers is best?

a. In analyzing an argument, we identify a proposition as a conclusion by preceding it with a 'C.' (Page 82)

b. In analyzing an argument, we identify a proposition as a premise by preceding it with a 'P'. (Page 106)

c. In analyzing an argument, we write the premise(s) above the conclusion. (Page 151)

d. More than one of the above answers are correct. (Page 171)

e. Answers (a) through (d) are all incorrect. (Page 128)

5.5 Answer (c)

This text expresses the argument—

        P. Louisiana is south of Arkansas.
        C. Louisiana is also south of Missouri.

—, to which the unexpressed premise 'Arkansas is south of Missouri' must be added. The argument that the author has in mind is deductive (we assume, in the absence of any expressions that tell us otherwise); and it is valid, inasmuch as the premises—expressed and unexpressed—jointly make the conclusion certain. Both the expressed and the unexpressed premises are not only asserted but true. Therefore, the argument, being valid and free of false asserted premises, is sound. Answer (c), then, is correct.

But is it the only answer that is correct? Return to page 75 to reconsider.

6.6 Answer (a)

'Must' seems here to be used as a redundant illative. For if 'must' were deleted, the other illative, 'shews [= shows] that', alone would indicate the same argument. But when 'must' is used as an illative, it tells us that the argument it indicates is verificatory. Answer (a), then, is incorrect.

Return to page 119 to try again.

1.7 Answer (e)

This is the correct answer. For, contrary to answer (c), the text contains an illative. But, contrary to answer (a), it isn't 'Furthermore': it is 'this fact that . . . leads to the conclusion that'. And, contrary to answer (b), that illative indicates the argument—

P. The material is indifferent to the division of time.
C. The lapse of time is an accident, rather than of the essence, of the material.

Even though you may not have a clear idea of what this argument means, thanks to the illative in the text, you can analyze it. Proceed to page 78 for the next question.

2.3 Answer (b)

This answer is correct. The text expresses the argument—

P. The common people are human beings.
C. The common people are sometimes inconstant.

(For details, see the commentary to answer (a).) But, as answer (b) says, this argument is defective: it does not present the needed connection between the common people's *being human beings* and their *being sometimes inconstant*. One or more unexpressed premises are needed to provide this connection. So, answer (b) is correct.

But is it the only answer that is correct? Return to page 118 to reconsider.

4.6 Answer (b)

'Therefore' and 'for' are illatives that do not tell us whether the arguer believes that his premises make his conclusion probable or certain. So, if they are the only expressions that indicate what the arguer thinks about the relation between his premises and conclusion, we cannot ascertain whether the argument is deductive or inductive by consulting the arguer's expressions. Answer (b), then, is incorrect.

Return to page 114 to try again.

1.9 Answer (a)

'Certainly' is not an illative, so that this answer is wrong. When someone says something of the form 'Certainly, *x*', as Aristotle does in this text, he tells us that he thinks that '*x*' is certain, but not that he thinks '*x*' is a premise or a conclusion of an argument.

After writing on your answer sheet a brief explanation why this answer is wrong, return to page 88 to try again.

3.8 Answer (e)

At least one of the answers (a) through (d) is correct, so that (e) is incorrect. Return to page 134 to try again.

5.11 Answer (a)

This answer is incorrect, because the premise 'There are powers less than oneself' does not confer certainty on the conclusion 'There is a power greater than oneself'. Given only that there are powers less than oneself, it remains possible that there is no power greater; for it remains possible that one is oneself the greatest power. Suppose God were to recite this argument to Himself. Should it persuade Him that there is a power greater than Himself? No, because even though there are powers less than Himself, it remains possible that there are none greater. The premise, then, does not make the conclusion certain. So, answer (a) is incorrect.

Return to page 104 to try again.

6.2 Answer (c)

It is true that the two propositions 'John's uncle advised him to take this job' and 'His uncle has never been wrong' could help to verify, but not explain, 'John ought to take this job'; for they provide some evidence that he ought to take the job but fail to explain why. It is also true that 'This job would offer John all the advantages he wants without any disadvantages' could help either to verify or to explain 'John ought to take this job'; for, if we did not already know that he ought to take the job, this proposition could be a reason for thinking that he should; and, if we already knew (*e.g.*, by consulting his unfailing uncle) that he ought to take the job, this proposition would help to tell us why. Therefore, answer (c) is correct.

But is it the best answer? Return to page 137 to try again.

1.12 Answer (c)

Tut, tut! We can do better than this. The text contains no illatives, so that we cannot consult them. That leaves us with the Aptitude Method. First, then, we must ask whether either of the propositions expressed in the text would plausibly be a reason for the other. If neither would, then (c) would be correct; but it's not. Given, then, that at least one of the propositions would plausibly be a reason for the other, we must find out whether each or only one would plausibly be a reason for the other.

Now, you take it from there. After writing on your answer sheet a brief explanation why this answer is wrong, return to page 80 to try again.

4.4 Answer (b)

'Probably' tells us that the author thinks that the proposition 'A being of higher faculties is capable of more acute suffering than one of an inferior type' is probable. But it does not tell us whether he believes that that proposition is a reason for anything else, or that anything else is a reason for it. Does any other expression tell us this? If not, can we learn it through the Aptitude Method? Only if the answer to one of these two questions is affirmative can we conclude that the text expresses an inductive argument.

Return to page 123 to try again.

5.10 Answer (b)

This answer is incorrect, since the premises jointly *do* make the conclusion certain: if strains of gonococci resistant to penicillin have been found in other places by other people (as the argument's premises claim), then Phillips' discovery of such a strain cannot be *unique*—i.e., the only one of its kind.

Return to page 59 to try again.

6.7 Answer (b)

This answer is incorrect, because the illative 'renders it probable that' does not tell us whether the argument that it indicates is verificatory or explanatory. For whether the author had in mind a verification or an explanation, he could still express himself by means of that illative.

Return to page 84 to try again.

1.4 Answer (d)

No more than one of the answers (a) through (c) are correct, so that (d) is incorrect. Return to page 121 to try again.

2.6 Answer (b)

The expressed argument, indicated by the illative 'because' is—

P. The King [Philip IV of Spain] wanted to have Italian fresco painters at court.
C. Velázquez tried to tempt Pietro da Cortona to Madrid.

This is obviously defective. For one thing, it fails to provide any connection between *Philip's court* and *Madrid*. Perhaps an unexpressed premise would help. Answer (b) suggests 'Philip's court was in Madrid'. This satisfies both requirements of the Method of Supply, and so it should be added. Answer (b), then, is correct.

But is it the best answer? Return to page 116 for another look.

4.8 Answer (b)

This answer is incorrect, because the word 'can't' is used here to help express the premise. It does not work together with 'consequently', nor does it in any way help to tell us whether the arguer believes that his premise makes his conclusion probable or certain. Therefore, we cannot ascertain whether the argument is deductive or inductive by consulting 'can't'. Answer (b), then, is incorrect.

Return to page 117 to try again.

5.8 Answer (c)

This answer is correct. The arguer thinks that his premise makes his conclusion certain (see commentary to answer (a), p. 120), but he is mistaken (see commentary to answer (b), p. 105); and consequently the argument is invalid, as answer (c) asserts.

But is this the only correct answer of the lot? Return to page 85 to find out.

1.8 Answer (a)

The two occurrences of the illative 'since' in this text work together, not separately. That is, together they indicate the same, single argument, rather than each one indicating a different argument. Consequently, the text expresses not two arguments but only one.

After writing on your answer sheet a brief explanation why this answer is wrong, return to page 78 to try again.

3.1 Answer (c)

Yes, this is one of the possibilities: the arguments may share the same conclusion but not the same premises. And so answer (c) is correct.

But is it the only answer that is correct? Return to page 130 to reconsider.

4.9 Answer (a)

'Cannot' and 'nor can' help to express premises, and so they have nothing to do with whether the arguer believes that his premises make his conclusion certain or probable. Hence, we cannot ascertain whether the argument is deductive or inductive by consulting these expressions. For this reason, answer (a) is incorrect.

Return to page 121 to try again.

5.3 Answer (c)

This answer is incorrect, because part of what it says is false. It says first that an argument may be valid without being sound, and that is true. (For details, see the commentary to answer (a), on page 145.) Next, it says that an argument may be sound without being valid; but that is false.

Return to page 114 to try again.

6.5 Answer (d)

No more than one of the answers (a) through (c) are correct, so that (d) is incorrect.
Return to page 126 to try again.

1.1 Answer (e)

This is the correct answer, as answers (a) through (d) are all incorrect. In the sense in which it is used in this book, the word 'argument' means a smallest unit of reasoning— *i.e.,* at least one reason given for something, together with the thing for which it is given— *i.e.,* at least one premise, together with a conclusion.

Proceed to the next question, on page 129.

3.4 Answer (a)

This answer is incorrect, because the text expresses at least two arguments that are unconnected. (That is, they do not share a premise, they do not share a conclusion, and neither's conclusion is the other's premise.)

Return to page 109 to try again. Analyze the arguments expressed in the text before trying to answer a question about their connectedness.

4.5 Answer (c)

It would not be proper merely to assume that the arguer believes that his premise makes his conclusion certain, as the text contains expressions that indicate whether he thinks his premise makes his conclusion probable or certain. Therefore, answer (c) is wrong.

Return to page 105 to try again.

5.2 Answer (b)

This answer is incorrect, because it confuses soundness with validity. If an argument's premises actually make its conclusion probable or certain, depending on which the arguer thinks they do, then the argument is valid. But more than that is needed to make an argument sound.

Return to page 122 to try again.

6.3 Answer (d)

No more than one of the answers (a) through (c) are correct, so that (d) is incorrect.
Return to page 138 to try again.

1.11 Answer (a)

The text contains no illative, but it may nevertheless express an argument. For an argument may be expressed by a text without illatives. And, as a matter of fact, this text does express an argument.

After writing a brief explanation why this answer is incorrect, return to page 90 for another try.

2.2 Answer (b)

This answer is incorrect, because a premise does not differ from a presupposition in that a premise may be either expressed or unexpressed, whereas a presupposition cannot be expressed. For a presupposition *can* be expressed.

After writing on your answer sheet a brief explanation why this answer is wrong, return to page 135 to try again.

EXERCISE SET 5

5.1 Question

An argument is valid if:

a. Its premises actually make its conclusion probable. (Page 173)

b. Its premises actually make its conclusion certain. (Page 158)

c. Its premises actually make its conclusion either probable or certain. (Page 79)

d. More than one of the above answers are correct. (Page 148)

e. Answers (a) through (d) are all incorrect. (Page 62)

6.1 Answer (c)

This is the correct answer. Answers (a) and (b) are incorrect because, unlike (c), they leave out of account what the arguer thinks about the relation between his premises and conclusion.

Advance to page 137 for the next question.

1.10 Answer (c)

This answer is incorrect, because the expression 'in all probability' is not an illative. For it does not tell us that the person who uses it thinks that one thing is a reason for another.

After writing a brief explanation why this answer is incorrect, return to page 68 for another try.

2.1 Answer (b)

This answer is incorrect, since it is not true that any unexpressed premise that we add to our analysis of an argument should plausibly assist any expressed premises to make the conclusion *certain*. For the author may not have intended his premises to make his conclusion certain. For example, the author of the text—

Socrates is probably right-handed, as he is a stonemason.

—, thinks that his premises make his conclusion 'Socrates is right-handed' not certain but only probable, as his use of the word 'probably' tells us. Consequently, we would not be completing the argument that the author had in mind if we were to add an unexpressed premise that, like 'All stonemasons are right-handed', would help the expressed premise to make the conclusion not probable but certain.

After writing on your answer sheet a brief explanation why this answer is wrong, return to page 160 to try again.

4.3 Answer (c)

This answer is incorrect, because the author *does* use at least one expression that tells us whether he thinks the premise makes the conclusion probable or certain.

Return to page 66 to try again.

5.7 Answer (b)

This answer is incorrect. Unfortunately, we cannot explain further without giving away too much.

Return to page 103 to try again.

1.6 Answer (c)

This answer is incorrect, because the Aptitude Method does not say that, in a text containing no illatives, whichever of the propositions expressed by the text is not likely to be disbelieved by the author is a premise in an argument.

After writing on your answer sheet a brief explanation why this answer is wrong, return to page 160 to try again.

EXERCISE SET 3

3.1 Question

When a text expresses more than one argument, it is possible that:

a. The text expresses only one of the arguments, the others remaining implicit. (Page 173)

b. The arguments share the same premises but not the same conclusion. (Page 82)

c. The arguments share the same conclusion but not the same premises. (Page 166)

d. More than one of the above answers are correct. (Page 143)

e. Answers (a) through (d) are all incorrect. (Page 158)

4.7 Answer (e)

At least one of the answers (a) through (d) is correct, so that (e) is incorrect. Return to page 89 to try again.

5.6 Answer (b)

The text does not express an inductive argument, valid or otherwise. Perhaps you overlooked the word 'certainly'.

Return to page 65 to try again.

1.3 Answer (d)

This is the correct answer, because answers (a), (b), and (c) are *all* correct. Proceed to page 121 for the next question.

4.6 Answer (a)

In this text, the word 'certainly' helps to express one of the argument's premises; it does not help to tell us whether the arguer believes his premises make his conclusion probable or certain. 'Certainly', then, cannot properly be consulted to ascertain whether the argument that the text expresses is deductive or inductive. For this reason, answer (a) is incorrect.

Return to page 114 to try again. And remember that, when ascertaining whether an argument is deductive or inductive, you consult not just any expressions that happen to be in the text but only those that indicate whether the arguer believes his premises make his conclusion probable or certain.

5.8 Answer (d)

There you go! Answers (a), (b), and (c) are all correct. The argument is deductive, as 'this shews that' and 'must' indicate; but its premise does not render its conclusion certain; and so the argument is invalid.

Proceed to page 74 for the next question.

6.6 Answer (e)

This is the correct answer, as all the others are wrong. The text expresses the argument—

P. The nests of hummingbirds and the playing passages of bowerbirds are tastefully ornamented with gaily colored objects.
C. These birds receive some kind of pleasure from the sight of such things.

—, as the illatives 'shews [= shows] that' and (redundantly) 'must' tell us. Each of these illatives tells us that the argument is both deductive and verificatory.

The next question is on page 84.

1.9 Answer (b)

It is true that 'Therefore' is an illative, that its occurrence in this text tells us that the text expresses an argument, and that it identifies 'Certainly all human things are incapable of continuous activity' as a premise, and 'Pleasure also is not continuous' as the conclusion, of that argument. But there is more to the argument than the analysis in answer (b) captures. Consequently, this is not the best answer.

After writing on your answer sheet a brief explanation why this answer is wrong, return to page 88 to try again.

4.5 Answer (a)

It is true that the text expresses an argument, that we ascertain whether it is deductive or inductive by consulting the author's expressions, and that we consult at least the illative 'therefore'. But it is not true that we consult the word 'certainly'. For it is part of the phrase 'probably, although *not* certainly' and so is used to help indicate that the writer has in mind probability *rather than* certainty. This is why we do not consult it and then conclude that the argument that the text expresses is deductive. Therefore, answer (a) is wrong.

Return to page 105 to try again.

5.9 Answer (c)

This answer is incorrect. The premise 'A two-year study of IHS found that only 22 of its 51 hospitals meet minimum accreditation standards, that only 16 of them meet national fire and safety codes, and that 19 should be replaced and 14 extensively modernized at a cost of $200 million' *has* a logical bearing on the conclusion 'Once they get there [IHS hospitals or clinics], Indians enter inadequate facilities': namely, the premise makes the conclusion more likely to be true than false. Answer (c), then, is wrong.

Return to page 74 to try again.

6.7 Answer (a)

This answer is incorrect, because the illative 'renders it probable that' does not tell us whether the argument that it indicates is verificatory or explanatory. For whether the author had in mind a verification or an explanation, he could still express himself by means of that illative.

Return to page 84 to try again.

1.8 Answer (c)

This answer is incorrect, as the text does not express the argument analyzed in answer (c): no illative points it out, and the Aptitude Method will not reveal it.

After writing on your answer sheet a brief explanation why this answer is wrong, return to page 78 to try again.

3.1 Answer (a)

This answer is incorrect, because if, as the question states, the text expresses *more than one* argument, then it cannot be the case that the text expresses *only one* of the arguments: it must express at least two of them. Hence, given what the question states, answer (a) cannot be correct.

Return to page 130 to try again.

5.1 Answer (a)

This answer is incorrect, because an *in*valid argument's premises may actually make its conclusion probable. For instance, if someone says—

> Most stonemasons are right-handed, and Socrates is a stonemason. From this it follows that Socrates is right-handed.

—, the premises of his argument—

      P1. Most stonemasons are right-handed.
      P2. Socrates is a stonemason.
      C. Socrates is right-handed.

—actually make its conclusion probable; and yet the argument is invalid.

Return to page 168 to try again.

6.8 Answer (c)

This answer is correct. But is it the only correct one?
Return to page 110 to try again.

1.7 Answer (d)

No more than one of the answers (a) through (c) are correct, so that (d) is incorrect. Return to page 70 to try again.

4.8 Answer (c)

This is the correct answer. The text expresses the argument—

      P. You can't explain anything by reasoning.
      C. It is useless to reason.

To ascertain whether this argument is deductive or inductive, we must simply assume that the arguer believes that his premises make his conclusion certain. For there are only two expressions in the text that might seem at first to have any bearing on the question: 'can't' and 'consequently'. The former helps to express the premise and so in fact has no bearing on whether the arguer thinks that very premise makes the conclusion probable or certain. The latter is an illative that does not say whether the author believes his premise makes his conclusion probable or certain. Therefore, we cannot rely on any expressions that the arguer uses and are compelled to consider the argument deductive.

Proceed to page 121 for the next question.

5.10 Answer (e)

All the other answers are wrong, so (e) is right. The argument is detectable only through the Aptitude Method. It is deductive, not for the reason given in answer (a), but because no expressions in the text tell us otherwise. Contrary to answer (b), the premises make the conclusion certain. Consequently, the argument is valid and deductive.

Proceed to page 104 for the next question.

6.5 Answer (a)

This answer is incorrect. Observe that Holmes asks Lestrade, "But *why* didn't the police see this mark yesterday?"

Return to page 126 to try again.

1.5 Answer (d)

No more than one of the answers (a) through (c) are correct, so that (d) is incorrect. Return to page 87 to try again.

4.4 Question

Text:

> A being of higher faculties requires more to make him happy, is capable probably of more acute suffering, and certainly accessible to it at more points, than one of an inferior type. . . .

—John Stuart Mill, *Utilitarianism* (1861), ed. Oskar Piest (Indianapolis: The Bobbs-Merrill Company, Inc., 1957), Ch. 2, p. 13.

This text expresses:

a. A deductive argument, as we properly discover by consulting the expression 'certainly'. (Page 154)

b. An inductive argument, as we properly discover by consulting the expression 'probably'. (Page 164)

c. A deductive argument. For the text contains the conflicting expressions 'probably' and 'certainly', so that we cannot profitably consult the expressions that the author uses. (Page 144)

d. More than one of the above answers are correct. (Page 93)

e. Answers (a) through (d) are all incorrect. (Page 103)

5.11 Answer (c)

This answer is incorrect, because the premise, though asserted, is not false but true. Assuming that by 'power' is meant something possessing a capacity for action, there are powers less than man—*e.g.,* sloths, slugs, and thistles.
Return to page 104 to try again.

INDEX OF WORKBOOK EXERCISES

1.1Q......... 81
A....... 157
B....... 120
C....... 97
D....... 144
E....... 167

1.2Q....... 129
A....... 159
B........ 93
C....... 143
D....... 113
E........ 64

1.3Q....... 161
A........ 82
B....... 106
C....... 151
D....... 171
E....... 128

1.4Q....... 121
A....... 138
B....... 148
C........ 69
D....... 165
E........ 99

1.5Q....... 87
A........ 98
B....... 158
C....... 147
D....... 175
E........ 76

1.6Q....... 160
A....... 102
B....... 111
C....... 170
D........ 86
E....... 149

1.7Q......... 70
A....... 140
B........ 94
C....... 124
D....... 174
E....... 162

1.8Q......... 78
A....... 166
B....... 145
C....... 173
D........ 92
E....... 156

1.9Q......... 88
A....... 163
B....... 172
C....... 112
D....... 127
E....... 153

1.10Q......... 68
A....... 139
B........ 84
C....... 169
D....... 146
E........ 96

1.11Q......... 90
A....... 168
B....... 154
C....... 133
D....... 100
E........ 71

1.12Q......... 80
A....... 107
B....... 152
C....... 164
D........ 95
E....... 132

2.1Q....... 160
A....... 117
B........ 72
C....... 131
D........ 92
E....... 150

2.2Q....... 135
A........ 87
B....... 168
C....... 110
D....... 100
E........ 76

2.3Q....... 118
A....... 142
B....... 162
C....... 107
D........ 93
E........ 64

2.4Q......... 91
A....... 109
B....... 143
C........ 77
D....... 120
E........ 99

2.5Q......... 97
A....... 113
B........ 66
C....... 130
D........ 86
E....... 149

2.6Q....... 116
A....... 125
B....... 165
C....... 155
D....... 102
E........ 82

3.1Q....... 130
A....... 173
B........ 82
C....... 166
D....... 143
E....... 158

3.2Q......... 98
A....... 112
B....... 136
C....... 125
D........ 86
E....... 148

3.3Q....... 115
A....... 131
B........ 99
C....... 120
D....... 146
E........ 87

3.4Q......... 109
A....... 167
B........ 93
C....... 129
D....... 150
E........ 64

3.5Q....... 122
A....... 106
B....... 156
C........ 74
D....... 142
E....... 132

3.6Q....... 108
A........ 95
B........ 83
C....... 144
D....... 127
E....... 159

3.7Q......... 72
A....... 128
B........ 92
C....... 113
D........ 61
E....... 138

3.8Q 134	**4.6Q** 114	**5.3Q** 114	**5.9Q** 74	**6.4Q** 76
A 100	A 171	A 145	A 144	A 141
B 124	B 162	B 124	B 91	B 111
C 153	C 135	C 166	C 172	C 128
D 76	D 92	D 82	D 160	D 156
E 163	E 150	E 156	E 116	E 99
4.1Q 94	**4.7Q** 89	**5.4Q** 83	**5.10Q** 59	**6.5Q** 126
A 128	A 159	A 147	A 152	A 174
B 104	B 113	B 106	B 164	B 154
C 146	C 148	C 119	C 138	C 86
D 156	D 74	D 127	D 92	D 166
E 64	E 170	E 159	E 174	E 144
4.2Q 101	**4.8Q** 117	**5.5Q** 75	**5.11Q** 104	**6.6Q** 119
A 127	A 155	A 140	A 163	A 161
B 115	B 165	B 151	B 137	B 82
C 152	C 141	C 161	C 175	C 108
D 138	D 63	D 128	D 149	D 93
E 82	E 100	E 113	E 86	E 171
4.3Q 66	**4.9Q** 121	**5.6Q** 65	**6.1Q** 149	**6.7Q** 84
A 147	A 166	A 157	A 134	A 172
B 132	B 136	B 170	B 123	B 164
C 169	C 153	C 126	C 168	C 120
D 99	D 106	D 146	D 106	D 132
E 120	E 86	E 99	E 92	E 96
4.4Q 123	**5.1Q** 168	**5.7Q** 103	**6.2Q** 137	**6.8Q** 110
A 154	A 173	A 76	A 101	A 145
B 164	B 158	B 169	B 153	B 85
C 144	C 79	C 93	C 163	C 71
D 93	D 148	D 64	D 65	D 155
E 103	E 62	E 150	E 127	E 100
4.5Q 105	**5.2Q** 122	**5.8Q** 85	**6.3Q** 138	
A 118	A 67	A 120	A 116	
B 151	B 167	B 105	B 90	
C 167	C 133	C 165	C 157	
D 71	D 153	D 71	D 64	
E 137	E 100	E 132	E 146	

RAW FOOD